Selling a California Business

The Ultimate Guide for California Business Owners!

Peter Siegel, MBA

Peter Siegel, MBA
Selling A California Business

This publication is designed to provide accurate and authoritative information with regard to the subject matter covered. It is sold with the understanding that the publisher is not engaged in rendering legal, accounting, or other professional advice. If legal advice or other expert assistance is required, the services of a competent professional should be sought.

Printed in the United States of America

ISBN: 0-9761985-0-9

Library Of Congress Control Number: 2004113203

Bulk Quantity Discounts:
This book and companion books from this publisher are available at quantity discounts for bulk purchases for educational, business or sales promotional use. For information regarding bulk purchases please call (800) 572-7260.

Publisher:
California Businesses For Sale / www.bizben.com
9110-B Alcosta Blvd., #238
San Ramon, CA. 94583
(800) 572-7260

Other books by Peter Siegel, MBA, available from this publisher:
Buying a California Business -
    The Ultimate Guide for Savvy Business Buyers!
Businesses For Sale -
    A Guide for Business Buyers, Business Owners & Business Brokers

See our website at: www.bizben.com

ACKNOWLEDGEMENTS

For the past 15 years, it has been my privilege to be associated with a number of creative, dedicated and talented people in my work as a business buyer, business seller, business broker and founder and president of a growing organization that facilitates the marketing of small businesses for sale throughout California.

I am indebted to a number of professionals, too numerous to mention, from whom I have gained the education and the inspiration, as well as the ideas and the insights which I endeavor to share with others on the pages of this book.

I am grateful for the opportunities I have had to learn and to grow in this fascinating and vital area of business.

Peter Siegel, MBA
January, 2005

Done correctly, the sale of your business can move you quickly in the direction you'd like your life to take. But if handled poorly, you may be letting yourself in for a series of unpleasant, even tragic experiences you'll long regret.

If you have unrealistic expectations or you're not willing to have your business carefully scrutinized - even criticized - you may not have the attitude required to sell successfully.

- ❖ The Reality Check
- ❖ Conform to Market (Not the Other Way Around)
- ❖ Be Forthcoming with Needed Information
- ❖ Demonstrating There's Nothing to Hide
- ❖ Do the Necessary Work
- ❖ Conclusion
- ❖ Key Points from this Chapter

Buyers want a business with a successful past and a promising future. Will yours pass the test?

- ❖ It's Not Real Estate
- ❖ Outside Factors: Viable Market and Demand
- ❖ The Business: Well Positioned and Equipped with Lease, Assets, Favorable Agreements, Ability, Transferability
- ❖ Examples of Adjustments Made to Achieve a Sale
- ❖ Surprises Murder Transactions
- ❖ Conclusion
- ❖ Key Points from This Chapter

Many sellers manage to pull together the obvious things needed to satisfy a buyer. It's the items you might not think about that are likely to sabotage your sale.

- ❖ What you Probably Thought of Already: Books/Records, Equipment List, Profile
- ❖ Staging
- ❖ Trial Run
- ❖ Assemble Your Team
- ❖ Why Half the Deals Fail
- ❖ What You May Not Have Anticipated: Meeting with Landlord, Approvals, Transfer of Licenses
- ❖ Do the Hard Work Now to Reap the Benefits Later
- ❖ Conclusion
- ❖ Key Points from This Chapter

Featuring the Successful bizben Method!

INTRODUCTION

The soft sands and tropical Tahitian breezes gently warm your skin as you enjoy a luscious fruit drink with shaved ice, and think about your major problem of the day: "Take a nap now and go to lunch later, or do it the other way around?"

That is the dream for some small business owners in California who believe that if they could sell the business for enough money, they could say "hello" to the good life, and "so long" to the challenges of meeting payroll, building sales, handling problem customers and dealing with all the other issues that keep coming up, one after the other, throughout each hectic day.

Whether it's the vision of Tahiti's beaches, the idea of pursuing another career, the desire for more time with family and hobbies, or simply the need to end the financial drain caused by the business, if you're contemplating putting the "for sale" sign on your enterprise, you should know that it could well be one of the most important moves in your life.

Done correctly, the sale of your business can move you quickly in the direction you'd like your life to take. But if handled poorly, you may be letting yourself in for a series of unpleasant, even tragic experiences you'll long regret.

It's the purpose of this book to help you avoid some of the pitfalls and mistakes that can be made in the difficult process of selling, so that you can happily embrace the next stage you see for your life.

Remember the sun block.

CHAPTER ONE

ARE YOU REALLY READY TO SELL?

If you are the owner of a small California business – that is, a business with a market value under $5 million, and with the majority selling for less than $1 million – you belong to an important group of Californians who provide employment for hundreds of thousands of people, contribute millions of dollars in tax revenues to federal, state and local governments, and play a vital role in supplying products and services in what is the world's sixth largest economy.

And chances are – based on the turnover rates of small businesses in California – that you either are currently trying to sell your business or will want to do so within the next five years.

If that's the case, you should realize that the majority of small California businesses on the market do not sell. In fact, only three out of ten small business offerings in this state result in a completed deal.

That's the bad news.

The other side of the coin is that most of those businesses that languish unsold on the market could be sold if the owners were truly committed to doing what is needed to effect a transaction at a fair price and terms.

In the following pages, you'll learn what it takes to sell your business, and you'll find plenty of advice to help you make that happen quickly and at the right terms.

And that begins with your attitude.

Like any worthwhile endeavor, your chance of success is highly dependent on your frame of mind. And so the first topic to address if you are contemplating the sale of your small California business – or even if you have already placed it on the market – is the set of assumptions by which you operate:

Do you think it will be a "red letter day" for California buyers when your small business hits the market? Do you envision people standing in line with wads of cash clamoring for your attention?

Or do you plan to assess the realities of the marketplace and prepare your offering accordingly?

Do you expect to dictate to buyers, intermediaries, and anyone else who'll listen, the strict terms you expect will be met by anyone lucky enough to bid on your business?

Or do you see the selling process as more of a collaborative effort involving a skilled broker, a qualified buyer, and your team of professionals?

Having examined literally hundreds of business offerings over the years, and observing those which resulted in a successful deal, as well as the majority, which turned out to be an exercise in frustration for sellers, brokers and would-be buyers, it's clear to me that the number one factor influencing the outcome of an attempted sale is the willingness of the California small business owner to sell.

My colleagues in the industry and I have seen any number of different situations and conditions that have prevented a business owner from achieving a sale. Yet in most cases, there has been one underlying problem: The reluctance of the seller to do what it takes to attract and satisfy a buyer interested in paying the going market rate and terms for the business.

The Reality Check

Before you start assembling books and records, talking to brokers, and doing the other things that are needed to get your enterprise on the market, let's begin with a simple exercise that will help you predict whether or not you'll be able to sell your business.

Take a few moments to review and answer the following questions as honestly as you can.

Are you willing to accept the market price for your business, rather than having a figure – usually higher than market value – in mind, and insisting on that figure as the selling price?

Are you prepared to do the tedious, sometimes difficult work of preparing your business for sale? That includes pulling together a lot of information and having serious conversations with your landlord, the franchisor (if applicable), and perhaps with employees and others.

Are you able to remain flexible throughout the process, changing your expected terms if you have the right buyer, but one who chooses to structure the deal in a different way than you'd anticipated? For example, even though you want an all-cash transaction, are you willing to finance a portion of the purchase price?

Are you willing to work cooperatively with experts in the field of business sales as they market your company, qualify buyers, manage negotiations, and advise about terms and conditions of a sale?

Are you prepared to work with prospective buyers who are analyzing your business before sale, and with the successful buyer afterward?

Are you able to view your business from the perspective of a buyer? If you were looking for a business to purchase, one meant to provide you a reasonable income based on your investment of money, time and labor, would you be interested in a business like yours?

If you can answer these questions with an honest "yes," it means you have a good chance of selling your business. If, however, you are not sure about the answers, or if you want to wait to "see what happens" when your business is offered to prospective buyers, it's likely you aren't prepared to make the commitment needed to achieve the status of "former owner.".

Conform to Market (Not the Other Way Around)

Unlike the real estate market, which is supported by a formal mechanism for determining values, the market for small businesses in California is highly fragmented, and heavily influenced by a number of internal and external factors. Rarely are two businesses alike. And even if they were, there is no public depository of information where selling prices and terms are recorded. Otherwise, anyone could access this data to make comparisons and determine a proper, comparable, value for a business.

A successful sales strategy in this environment begins with a determination of what buyers are seeking, and then making sure that what you have to offer conforms to those requirements. This is particularly applicable in the case of price and terms, but also when it comes to training, covenant not to compete and some of the other particulars of a sale, as will be explored in the chapters to follow.

The best way to find out what multiples of earnings to apply in arriving at a price for a business like yours, or what valuation approaches are used to assess business assets, is to discuss this with a business broker or agent. Or you can consult with an appraiser familiar with valuing small businesses in California. And a second opinion is helpful. With information about the value of your business, given current market conditions, you are prepared to bring to market an offering that reflects today's realities.

Be Forthcoming with Needed Information

For many owners who've developed the habit of maintaining some secrecy about business affairs, it would be easier to give up a couple of teeth rather than share with others the details about their operations. Perhaps this describes you.

Naturally, it's important to limit exposure of the company to those prospective buyers who appear to be qualified as to ability, financial strength and interest. And we'll treat the subject of qualifying buyers in a subsequent chapter.

But once you've identified, and are dealing with a party who is a suitable candidate to be your buyer, it's to your advantage to open the books, candidly discuss matters that may not be reflected in your statements, and answer questions as honestly and completely as possible.

There may be some tidbits of information, such as the fact that your rent is due for an increase, or that a competitor is moving into the neighborhood, which you may prefer not to disclose. But all material facts are going to come out during the buyer's period of due diligence anyway. It's better that you volunteer whatever you know that might adversely affect the value and desirability of the business rather than have the buyer discover it later. If you make sure that you are the bearer of bad news, the prospective buyer is less likely to worry that you are hiding information. That's a worry that would prompt him or her to continue digging for negative facts. And by observing your candor, the buyer is more likely to believe you when you deliver "good news" about, for example, the new clients obtained, or the price reduction on needed supplies.

Sellers who fear that sharing negative information with a buyer might ruin a transaction, are reminded that if that is the case – if the deal is not going to work because of what you disclose – it's better to learn about that now and let the deal go. Otherwise, you would go through negotiations and the due diligence exercise, only to have things fall apart after days or weeks of work, and after your hopeful anticipation of a sale to the person. And you would squander, on a dead deal, valuable time that is better spent focusing on soliciting and working with other, more promising offers.

Your full and complete honesty about the circumstances – good and bad – of your small California business should start with the broker or agent, if you select one to represent you in the sale. Your intermediary would be severely hampered in his or her ability to do a good job for you if not prepared with all of the needed information.

Demonstrating There's Nothing to Hide

One of my broker associates tells the story about the seller of a catering company in Northern California who felt she was required to perform above and beyond the limits of normal disclosure. The buyer, as part of his examination of books and records, requested that she provide her entire personal tax returns for the prior three years, not just the Schedule Cs, which list the company's income and expenses and attach to the tax returns.

The seller felt that the personal tax return filed jointly with her husband and reflecting his salary as well as their income from a small trust left by a deceased relative, was simply none of the buyer's business.

The business broker encouraged her to cooperate because the buyer seemed well qualified, financially able and motivated to make the purchase. The broker explained that the buyer had experienced unpleasant surprises in the purchase of a café years before. Apparently, the buyer felt he might have avoided the problem had he scrutinized a more complete set of records than those provided. So he wanted everything he could see related to the catering company.

The seller finally agreed, stating that she had "nothing to hide." And once the buyer satisfied himself that indeed, everything was as she'd represented, he signed off on the contingencies, delivered his final check to escrow and closed the deal.

Though it seemed an unreasonable request, the seller was glad she'd complied, as it helped bring a good transaction to a successful conclusion.

Do the Necessary Work

"That seems like a lot of work," is a common sentiment of many owners when they learn what is required to prepare their small California business for sale. The next thought they have is: "I think I'll just wait till I get an interested party, then I'll start getting my information together."

For someone unfamiliar with the process of selling a small business, this might seem a reasonable strategy.

But it's a mistake! And the consequence is likely to be lost selling opportunities at a crucial time.

The initial 30 to 60 days after a business is placed on the market represent the most critical period. That is the valuable time that should be spent introducing interested and qualified buyers to the offering, providing them a complete package, answering their questions, soliciting offers, negotiating over details of any offers and handling the matters related to these steps.

Most every professional business broker has learned – the hard way – about the consequences of not being prepared for a sale when an interested party shows up asking questions and requesting information.

It typically takes two or three weeks, sometimes longer, to fully prepare a selling prospectus, determine what licenses and permits need to be transferred and start that ball rolling, and if necessary, negotiate with landlord, employee(s), and others whose cooperation will be important for a successful sale.

If that activity occurs while a buyer is waiting for information, for answers to questions and for the loose ends to be tied up, it's very likely the buyer will become interested in another offering or simply grow tired of remaining "on hold." That's why smart sellers are ready when their offering comes on the market.

Besides, doesn't it seem that a buyer will be more impressed with the quality of your business if you are able to present a complete package as soon as requested? Your professionalism and preparation reflects well on your sense of organization and your business abilities. And that suggests, in turn, that your business is well organized, efficiently run and worth purchasing.

Your role, of course, doesn't end with the preparatory activity. Even if you are represented by a broker or agent, you should plan on spending the time and the effort needed to work with buyers during the due diligence process and through the training period after the sale.

Conclusion

It's estimated that 70% of small businesses offered for sale in California are never sold, and that half of the accepted offers on these enterprises do not result in a completed deal. These aren't encouraging statistics for someone who wants to sell a small California business. But you can beat those odds and vastly improve the chances of enjoying a successful sale at a fair price and terms, if you are willing and ready to prepare for the marketing process, react to market feedback and cooperate fully with buyers and your representative during and even after the sale.

KEY POINTS FROM THIS CHAPTER

❖ *About 70% of small business owners in California who attempt to sell are unable to find a buyer at their price and terms.*

❖ *To improve these odds, it helps to be truly committed to the task of selling your business.*

❖ *See the Reality Check for some ideas about how to determine whether you're ready to sell.*

❖ *Determine what are the market realities and prepare your offering accordingly.*

❖ *Be forthcoming with needed information, the good news as well as the bad.*

❖ *Surprisingly, a buyer can be reassured when told, up front, about factors that may negatively affect a business. If the information does not discourage the person from buying the business, one benefit of revealing the facts is that the buyer will be more likely to believe you when you talk about the positive factors.*

❖ *And if disclosing negative information about your business is going to discourage some buyers, it's better to find that out at the beginning of negotiations, so as not to have them waste your time.*

❖ *An example of a seller who was forthcoming is the owner of a catering business who shared her personal tax returns, although reluctantly, with the buyer. Once satisfied that the seller had nothing to hide, the buyer completed the deal.*

❖ *Contrary to the ideas of many sellers, the right time to assemble the materials and create the selling prospectus is not after, but before the details are requested by an interested buyer.*

❖ *A successful sale is more likely to occur for those business owners who do the hard work of preparing their business materials and information, and dealing, beforehand, with any issues that need to be resolved.*

CHAPTER TWO

WHAT EXACTLY HAVE YOU GOT TO SELL?

It was noted in the previous chapter that if you want to sell your small California business, it helps if your offering conforms to the market. To use the expression of a traveling salesman from the last century: "You gotta find out what they're buying and that's what you sell 'em."

This idea is so obvious that it hardly seems worth expressing. And yet the failure by 70% of small business owners in California to find a buyer for their company can usually be tied in some way to the fact that this simple principal is forgotten or ignored.

The objective in this chapter is to help you understand from the buyer's perspective, what you have to sell. Once armed with that point of view, you'll be better equipped to offer your business in a way that increases the chances of its acceptance by a ready, willing and able buyer.

It's Not Real Estate

One common error made by sellers of small businesses in California is their overestimate of the intrinsic value represented by their offering. A seller often tries to assess his business in the same way he does his home.

But this is not an accurate comparison. Your home – most any real property for that matter – has a value that is reasonably constant and rooted in centuries-old reverence for the worthiness of the land. You don't have to do anything in your house for it to retain all or most of its value.

By contrast, your business is a dynamic entity, highly subject to a variety of influences and forces, inside and out. Its value can change very quickly.

As an example, consider the San Francisco restaurant that was purchased for nearly $1 million in 1999, then closed a year later after a dramatic decline in business due to the downturn in the dot.com economy. Once the disappointed owners had sold off their kitchen equipment and furnishings – receiving about ten cents per dollar of original asset value – then paid the penalty for early cancellation of their lease, there was nothing left to show for their investment.

When a buyer looks at the ever-changing package of risk and reward represented by what you have to offer, he or she may see the potential in your list of faithful, happy customers. And the buyer will be reassured if your business records show solid profits that were earned by serving these customers in the past.

The buyer also will imagine the downside: The fact that without those customers, without your experienced guidance and the work of your skilled employees, your business is merely a collection of equipment and inventory. And if those hard assets are not engaged in the conduct of the business, they will be stacked in the corner gathering dust, barely worth the cost of hauling them away.

Outside Factors: Viable Market and Demand

Most likely, the demand for what your business provides is as important as how you supply it. And, generally speaking, the greater the demand in the markets you serve, the more appeal your business will have for potential buyers.

If you think about this principal you'll understand why, for example, an owner of a sewing store in Southern California had difficulty selling his business. Yes, he still had an investment, representing thousands of dollars, in threads, fabrics, needles and supplies. And he'd certainly enjoyed several profitable years during the time when women tended to remain at home with kids, and could make a set of drapes in an afternoon. That's when the business supported the seller and his family, and provided the funds needed to send two sons to college.

But telling prospective buyers about those good old days did not help him achieve a sale of his business in the 21st Century.

There are numerous examples of this phenomenon. Changes in technology, population movement from cities to suburbs and back to renewed urban areas, and different habits of consumption, work, travel, leisure and entertainment have all impacted most every industry.

When examining your business from the viewpoint of a potential buyer, the first thing to look at critically is the marketplace in which you conduct your business.

Surprisingly, a number of sellers are oblivious to the realities around them, as was the owner of the sewing shop. Maybe they are suffering from self denial. In many cases they probably fear that if they admit to the decline in demand for the output of their business they'll scare away any interested buyers.

The Business: Well Positioned and Equipped with Assets, Favorable Agreements, Ability and Transferability

And if some business owners appear out of touch with the environment surrounding their enterprise, even more are disconnected from reality when they try to assess the workings of their business and its ability to respond to the market.

When applied to the outside factors, the question "what exactly have you got to sell?" addresses the strength of the marketplace in which your business functions. When applied to the internal factors, it requires that you look honestly and seriously at the ability of your company to do enough profitable business in that marketplace to be successful.

If there are factors preventing – or likely to prevent – your business from keeping up its level of good performance into the future, some of the prospective buyers for your business will catch onto these factors. You may not see these problems, or may not agree that they threaten the business. In either event, the difference between your perception of what you have to sell, and the view of the buyers about your offering, will account for the fact that you won't see purchase offers that match your requests for price and terms. Only by adjusting your vision to match that of people who might purchase your business, will you be able to understand what it takes to achieve a successful transaction. In other words, put yourself in the place of your prospective buyers so you can see your business through their eyes, and understand what it might take to meet their needs.

Some Examples of Adjustments Made to Achieve a Sale

Here, from my experience are some examples of businesses sufficiently affected by negative internal factors that they were difficult to sell. These situations include a few in which the sellers were able to honestly critique what they were offering and to adjust for the marketplace so as to attract serious buyers.

A dress shop in Central California had a good reputation and location but a short time remaining on its lease. At first, the seller felt this issue was not a problem because the store had been at the same corner for a long time. However, the prospective buyer noticed changes in the area, with new buildings going up and new uses for old properties. She felt these changes would reduce the likelihood of keeping the store in its familiar location at a reasonable rent. Once parties concurred that the lease should be removed from the deal – in other words, the business sale included the trade name, customer list and some inventory – they were able to arrive at a satisfactory agreement. With fewer assets in play, the seller realized the need to lower her price. The buyer, not having to pay the original asking price, was able to afford to finance a move to another location and to fund the promotion required to reintroduce the business to customers and announce its new store.

A man in contract to purchase a Southern California metal plating and finishing company made an interesting discovery while conducting his due diligence investigation. He learned that changes in local environmental regulations would prohibit the transfer of permits needed to operate the acid tanks used in the business. One of the lawyers involved in the deal came up with a solution. He proposed changing sale terms by eliminating the tanks from the list of equipment involved. Instead, they would be leased to the buyer by the seller, who would remain the owner of the tanks, thereby avoiding any necessity for a license transfer. The seller agreed to a reduction in the overall price because the buyer would receive less equipment in the deal, and would have the added expense of leasing the tanks. The buyer then asked for a more substantial discount in the sale price of the business. The reasoning was that it would be nearly impossible for the buyer to ever sell the business because of the license transfer problem. He argued that this factor reduced the value of the business. The seller refused to lower the price further and the transaction was aborted.

The owner of an appliance repair shop in a suburb of San Jose wanted to retire but was unable to find a buyer for his business. He ran a profitable enterprise with contracts to do warranty work with a number of manufacturers. The seller bragged that no one in that part of California, except he and his employee, was experienced and skilled enough to perform the repairs. And he claimed that's why the business was so successful. What frightened prospective buyers was the risk that the key employee might leave, and there would be no one in the business able to handle the work. After conferring with his business broker and attorney, the seller added a provision to his offering. He would remain in the business for a month to train the new owner. And if the employee were to leave within a 12-month period following close of escrow, the seller would go to work for the buyer, at the employee's salary, for the remainder of the one-year period. Within a few days of announcing this change, the broker was able to present two purchase offers and a deal was closed a month later.

The owner of a Northern California service bureau that worked for several large, prestigious ad agencies, decided to sell his business and retire. After the second accepted deal fell apart during the buyer's examination, the seller conferred with industry experts to discuss the problem. He realized that the desktop publishing revolution meant that most anyone with a personal computer and a graphics program could do much of their own work in preparing images for printing. Fewer of his services would be needed in the future. After some thought and analysis, the owner recognized that much of his expensive optical equipment was becoming obsolete. No wonder he couldn't find a buyer! So he removed his business from the market and went to work changing the focus of the company so it would be more in line with modern technology. It took six months to sell off old equipment, lease state-of-the-art systems and introduce a new range of digital graphic services for his clients. Then the seller reintroduced his business for sale, asking that a buyer pay him for goodwill–the company name and customer list – and assume the equipment leases. A successful transaction was completed in a few weeks.

Surprises Murder Transactions

These are examples of the work of some clever deal makers able to wrestle a victory out of the strong arms of defeat. One lesson behind these stories is that these offerings needed to be modified to correspond with the realities of the market, in order for the businesses to stand a chance of getting sold. Another important lesson is that these last-minute maneuvers are really the moves that should have been made when the businesses were first placed on the market. For every flawed business offering that gets fixed at the eleventh hour (and blessed with enough good fortune to save a deal that was doomed), there probably are ten instances when a business for sale that makes poor economic sense cannot be successfully sold. In other words, if you look at your business from the viewpoint of a rational buyer functioning in today's market, and you can't see a clear and solid way to make it pay off – considering the way you've got the deal structured – it's not likely that your efforts will result in a sale. But don't wait till the business has been on the market for several weeks before you decide to offer it in a way that is appealing, with a price drop or restructured down payment. And don't wait till a good buyer finds out about problems in your offering and refuses to go forward.

Because surprises murder transactions, the two-step strategy to increase your chances of completing a deal with your imperfect business (virtually all small California businesses have weaknesses) is to 1) disclose any problems with your business at the outset, and 2) have the offer put together in a way that allows a buyer of the business to deal with the challenges and still be successful.

Conclusion

If – in the words of the 20th Century traveling salesman – "They ain't buyin' what you're sellin'", when you place your small California business on the market, you'd be smart to take another look at what you are selling. See how it compares with the demands and desires among business buyers. If the marketplace in which your business operates is not continuing to support your enterprise, there may be little you can do to maintain a healthy business, let alone find an interested buyer.

But a business offering package often can be structured to accommodate a sale if its owner is flexible and applies realistic thinking and creative solutions to the problem.

KEY POINTS FROM THIS CHAPTER

❖ *Disagreement between buyer and seller as to what, of value, is for sale, is a key factor in the inability of 70% of the small businesses owners in California to find a buyer.*

❖ *Evaluate the outside factors impacting your business, such as demand for what you offer. If the market for the output of your company has declined, it will negatively affect the desirability of your business on the part of buyers. Sellers often are reluctant to face up to this problem.*

❖ *Looking honestly at internal factors influencing your business, and its ability to respond to the needs of its markets, will help you determine how the offering is seen by prospective buyers.*

❖ *Putting yourself in the place of possible buyers, and attempting to see your company through their eyes, is a very useful way to determine what it might take to attract offers.*

❖ *Factors that can make a business seem undesirable – but might be corrected – include lease problems, licenses and permits needed to operate, dependence on a key employee and outmoded technology.*

❖ *If negative factors at work in your business are discouraging offers, talk to advisors to determine what steps you can take to restructure it, or change the way it is offered, in order to make it more appealing to business buyers.*

❖ *Some of the ideas for overcoming problems that make your business unsalable include reducing the price, changing the terms, training the buyer for an extended period and altering the mix of assets included in the deal.*

❖ *Because surprises murder transactions, a seller is well advised to anticipate any problems with a business that might hurt its chances of getting sold, and then make sure the deal is structured in such a way that the offer remains appealing.*

CHAPTER THREE

PREPARATION

Most seasoned California business brokers will tell you that the initial appearance of your small business when it comes up for sale on the market can determine whether or not things will go well as it is reviewed and considered by potential buyers. Making a good first impression is vital. Just as important is that it can stand up under scrutiny.

Potential purchasers are quick to dismiss any offering that doesn't seem to pass muster. After all, the purchase of a business can be among the most important decisions in a person's life. At risk may be their life savings, along with the years of work and sacrifice devoted to succeeding in the business and securing their financial well being. A mistake can be disastrous.

Is it any wonder then, that a typical buyer is cautious, skeptical, even a bit cynical when looking at a seller's business and hearing the seller's claims?

In addition to exercising some healthy cynicism, buyers usually apply logic, working out the arguments for and against their acquisition of what you offer. They even use a bit of intuition as they examine various small business opportunities and consider what might be a good fit.

"Could I really do this?" "How does this feel?" "Are these people being honest with me?" These are some of the questions that pop into the buyer's mind, demanding answers, before he or she wants to go forward in the investigation of a possible acquisition.

You may notice that a prospective buyer is listening and asking questions, but also looking intensely around your office, and the facility, eager to observe any clues and collect any information that can be gleaned about the business. And as the buyer's questions come out, it may feel to you more like an interrogation than a question and answer session, with the prospect prepared to catch you in a misstatement.

So if you make a claim that you can't support, even if the failure results from an honest error; or if you subject someone to a process of due diligence that goes on too long and is too complicated, even if the facts are all there, you may wind up scaring away a good buyer. Forever.

And for no reason other than the fact that you weren't prepared.

That means the time to resolve problems and answer questions that might surface – to iron out any kinks in the offering – is before the first buyer has a chance to review it. Don't wait till you're well into the process.

As one broker puts it: "Once you start back pedaling, you're in trouble."

Even though we're not yet talking in detail about the stage where you're meeting with buyers – that part comes later in the book – it's important that sellers understand from the beginning, how critical it is that you are fully prepared when your enterprise goes on the block.

Rather than drag out your offering over a period of several months, changing the price every so often, and waiting for buyer comments and questions before deciding what information to collect and present, it's best to consider that you have a brief window to strut your business stuff. In my experience, the first 30 to 60 days after a small California business goes on the market may be the most critical time.

Here's a review of some of ways you can be prepared when your business is introduced for sale.

What You Probably Thought of Already: Books/Records, Equipment List, Profile

Books/records

Most buyers of small businesses in California feel that a three year financial history is sufficient to gain a solid understanding about the company's recent performance. Along with a P & L and balance sheet covering the prior three calendar or fiscal years, it's advisable to provide this information for the current year, as up to date as possible.

Depending on the size of the business and sophistication of the market in which it functions, you may be wise to provide audited financials or a review. The cost ($20,000 to $50,000) is an unneeded expense if you are selling a business at a price under about $1 million. And you probably won't be asked for audited numbers if your enterprise is in an industry about which there is a great deal of standard information available, so a buyer can readily determine if the performance of your business is typical. Additionally, audited records are generally not needed if you are selling a franchised business. The operating figures you provide to the franchisor are generally considered reliable reports, particularly if the buyer has the opportunity to talk with the franchisor, and verify numbers from your operation.

As the asking price gets close to $1 million and beyond, however, it's more likely that your buyers will want to know that your operating statements have been audited. That's because of the larger sums at stake, because the buyer for a business that size is likely to be more sophisticated and accustomed to reviewing audited information, and also because the audit cost is a small factor compared with the amount you stand to collect in a sale.

An audit might also be called for if your business is involved in the hi-tech sphere, utilizing some complicated accounting procedures to track, for example, licensing income or write-offs covering patents and certain kinds of agreements.

Simpler and less costly businesses usually can be properly represented, to the satisfaction of most buyers, with figures compiled as a result of an accounting review.

While buyers initially are provided with P & Ls and balance sheets covering three years, you may be asked, as you get into a sales agreement, to furnish the level of detail that allows buyers to verify the accuracy of your numbers. That means a seller is well advised to be ready to produce invoices, sales reports, accounts receivables aging schedules and other documentation that goes into the entries contained in your month-end reports.

Other supporting documents, such as depreciation schedules, payroll records and bank registers might also be requested and should be made available. But all of this detail is too much for an initial introduction of your business and we'll get to the way to "stage" the information later in this chapter.

Assets list

The depreciation schedule is a great place to start if you're assembling a list of equipment. You want to include all of your capital equipment, as well as office furniture, fixtures, and even leasehold improvements. Pull as much information together as possible, including acquisition cost and date, service contracts and records, and even appraisals. A used equipment dealer involved in your industry may be willing to give you some idea of valuation at a nominal cost.

Any vehicles to be included in the sale can be listed separately, showing their Blue Book value, mileage, accessories and so forth.

While it's a good idea to conduct an inventory of parts, supplies and finished goods at the outset, you can do it quickly to get an approximate value. A more detailed inventory will probably be conducted at close of escrow when the exact dollar value is required.

Copies of your lease – or leases if there are multiple locations – customer contracts, franchise agreements, deals established with employees and similar documentation can be considered assets of the business as well. These should be assembled and photocopied for presentation to a prospective buyer at the appropriate time.

Business Profile

How long has your enterprise been in business? How long have you owned it? How many employees? How many years remaining on the lease, and at what rental? These and other basic facts about the business should be presented in a one or two-page profile, also called "sell sheet" that can be shown to interested buyers as a first step in the introduction of your business.

Some business owners feel competent to prepare this document themselves while others feel it's worth a few hundred dollars to have this material prepared by a professional copy writer. And many business sellers, brokers and agents believe it's useful to add a page that describes the market in which your business functions, with an emphasis on the growth prospects. Back this up with any recent newspaper or trade magazine articles that talk about the glowing future of your industry and the growth anticipated in the market for your products and services. Such outside materials add credibility to your positive projections.

A one-page summary of your company's financial performance belongs with this package. It needn't go into the details of operations, just review the income, as up to date as possible for the current year, as well as for prior years, and a recount of the totals in the main categories of expenses. Balance sheet summaries can also be included.

Many business brokers encourage their clients or even help them, to prepare a page of "recast" financials. If you notice expense items that would not be incurred by a new owner (such as your car lease and country club membership), and if you feel that your successor – more active in the business than you are – could operate with lower labor costs, this is the place to document the dollar value of these differences. Show how the bottom line will be increased by adding back your personal expenses and deducting those costs that you have, but that need not accrue to the buyer.

Incidentally, while I think that recasting financials is a powerful tool in presenting a business to a prospective buyer, I fear its misuse in the way it is conveyed to the buyer. Be sure to include a disclaimer on the same page that describes the recast financial information. Note that the recast is your opinion not a representation or promise that the buyer will enjoy exactly the financial results depicted.

Another section of this profile might be a description of the ideal buyer. Suppose you use your electrical engineering experience in your business, and you recommend that the new owner have much the same background. A prospect who is similarly qualified may be more intrigued upon learning about this. And a prospect who lacks the capability will decline to pursue your offering, saving you time in the process.

And, as noted above, if you're aware of negative factors that might affect the future of your enterprise, it's advisable to state them in writing on a page called "disclosure notice." As we'll see, this page needn't be generally circulated, but should be available for judicious use.

For a useful tool that can help you put together an effective business profile, go to this Internet address: **www.bizben.com/selling-buying-business-forms.php**, and download the Business Profile form.

Staging

Of course, just because you've assembled all of this material and information does not mean you're required to hand it to everyone who thinks they may have an interest in your business. Rather, the common procedure is to distribute this data in "stages," matching the interest level of a prospective buyer with a suitable amount of information.

In Stage One, a buyer learns about the availability of your business and can have preliminary questions addressed with a single page "blind" profile, a form that reviews some of the particulars but does not include the name of your company or any identifying details.

If this sparks further interest on the part of the buyer, the next step is usually to obtain a signature on a non-disclosure agreement, whereby the buyer pledges to respect and observe the confidentiality of any information about your offering that is provided.

The Stage Two materials, for those who've signed non-disclosure agreements, can include the profile on the business along with a one or two-page summary of your company's financial information for the past three years. This might also be a good time to release the "disclosure notice" mentioned above, so the buyer is formally informed about any possible problems you anticipate in the future operation of the business.

Stage Three information is typically everything else that a buyer may want to see, but is predicated on an accepted offer, or at least an acceptable letter of intent for the buyer to purchase your business.

At this stage – the time for what is called "due diligence" – the buyer will have gained a fairly thorough overview about your business and will want to look into the specifics to deepen his or her understanding. The due diligence analysis is also the buyer's opportunity to verify the accuracy of the information provided in the earlier stages.

The buyer may engage the services of an accountant to go over the financials in more detail and compare your daily records with the summary contained in the balance sheets and profit and loss reports. Also, an attorney may be asked to review your property lease and other contracts and agreements. The purpose of this investigation is to make certain there are no undisclosed problems which the buyer feels will negatively impact the business in the future. The buyer's examination of these documents is also intended to verify that the information provided in earlier stages is supported by the detailed records.

Trial Run

In the process of preparing your business profile and organizing your financial information and other documents, you might want to pretend that you are a prospective buyer and actually go through a session of your own due diligence. Is every statement made in the business profile supported by the documentation? When the buyer reviews the financials, will materials such as the receivables aging reports, the payroll ledgers and the check register yield the exact same information as reported on the summaries?

If there are discrepancies, this is the time to become aware of them and make sure you have a correct explanation, or make changes to the profile so it corresponds to the facts.

Without the preparatory step of a trial run, you may be surprised to learn that inconsistencies exist in your reporting – inconsistencies which will be uncovered by the buyer. And while you're scratching your head and saying: "Gee, I didn't know about that," the buyer is likely to begin wondering if there are other "surprises," perhaps better hidden than what was uncovered. That's usually the moment when the buyer experiences a sense of distrust that can easily culminate in a "no sale".

Assemble Your Team

The final step in the category of obvious preparations is to make sure you have your experts in place, ready to help you when needed. As noted above, you might call on your attorney to review and discuss your lease or other agreements. And your accounting professional will be helpful in preparing a presentation of recast financial information. It may also be useful to obtain a business valuation from a qualified business broker or appraiser. And perhaps you'll engage an advertising expert to help plan your marketing campaign and to prepare the business profile that goes into the selling package (the collection of materials presented to interested and qualified buyers).

Why Half the Deals Fail

Poor preparation is a key factor in the failure that occurs in about 50% of deals that begin with an accepted offer.

Following the advice offered earlier in this chapter will help you prevent a number of these problems, by eliminating any surprises the buyer might encounter when moving into the due diligence phase of a transaction. Though initially skeptical, most buyers become more trusting if they discover consistency in the information as their examination of business records proceeds. And that's a healthy sign that your deal is going to hold together through completion.

But the preparation and assembly of written material and documentation is only half your job as you get your business ready for sale.

What You May Not Have Anticipated: Meeting with Landlord, Approvals, Transfer of Licenses

Even a profitable, well run business with impeccable records can be rejected by buyers and ignored by business brokers if all of the components needed to operate cannot be included in the sale. Sometimes it is just simple things – not handled on a timely basis – that ruin the chances for a healthy small California business to get matched up with a qualified and willing buyer.

Lease

An estimated twenty five percent of would-be business sales agreements have smashed up on the rocks over the past few years at the very point that a seller took a buyer to meet the land owner. And that doesn't factor in the cases in which the problems at that juncture were actually resolved, and the deal saved by a renegotiated lease or restructured deal – usually costly to the seller.

For retail businesses, including restaurants and many personal service enterprises, location is a key component of success. If there is a short time remaining on the lease and little likelihood of getting a new rental agreement or extension of the current one, the business will have little market value. Certainly the enterprise is worth much more with a long term lease in place than a short one. The saleability of a location-dependent operation is also impacted if the landlord chooses – and has legal standing – to withhold consent to assignment of the leasehold interest from seller to buyer.

Sellers of location-sensitive businesses certainly understand the importance of a good lease. Yet often they're reluctant to work to insure that they'll be able to satisfy this requirement in their offering.

"It's too early to talk to the landlady," is a typical comment. "Let's see if we get a good buyer, then we'll deal with the lease," is another.

And it's somewhat understandable that a business owner is reluctant to open the issue. There's the concern that talking to the landlord will force the cat out of the bag, causing the rumor mill to work overtime with discussions about exactly the topic which the seller would like to keep confidential – that is, the fact that the business is up for sale.

Then there's the worry that once your landlord knows you're planning to leave, he'll somehow feel betrayed, with the result of worsened relations between business owner and landlord. As any business operator knows, you've got enough troubles running a successful company without adding the problem of bad relations with the person to whom you send the monthly rent checks.

Despite these and related concerns, however, the best strategy invariably is to discuss your plans with the landlord before the business is officially on the market. Even if there's a major portion of eternity remaining on the lease, and a clear formula setting the rent well into the future, you should contact the person who owns the property where you conduct your business. Let her know there may be a new tenant in her future. Get her reaction. If she's got problems with that idea, work with her to get the issues resolved.

Will the new business owner need to meet a minimum standard of experience and financial solvency to satisfy the landlord? What is that standard? Are you going to have to remain on the lease and pay the rent if the buyer falls behind? Are you willing to do that? Do you need to get your lawyer involved to make sure you have solid rights of assignability under the lease? Will it take legal action to enforce those rights? Is that a cause you are willing to pursue?

It is these and similar questions that need to be posed so the solutions are incorporated into the business offering when it goes on the market. For example, a poor lease may mean the business is offered with a low down payment, so the buyer can retain some of the capital needed to finance a move.

Though it's tempting and it seems reasonable to put off the frustrating exercise of lease negotiations until it's an absolute must – when a specific buyer is waiting for the outcome, that's actually the worst time. While the buyer is wondering when there might be some resolution, he or she is likely to have second thoughts. That's when buyers typically find another business that is all ready to be taken over. You can eliminate those risks by working out the lease details beforehand.

Having lease terms spelled out applies even if you own the property and plan to keep it, leasing some or all to the new business owner. Establish the terms of the lease you want to provide. Then make them part of the package.

And if you own your business as a franchisee, with the lease belonging to the franchisor, your job is somewhat simplified. In most cases the approval from franchise head-quarters for you to proceed with your sale will include an okay for the lease transfer to an acceptable buyer.

Other agreements

The idea of having things worked out from the time the business goes on the market should be applied also to equipment leases, employment contracts, franchise obligations, purchase agreements covering your equipment, deals with customers, advertising orders and any other written – sometimes even verbal – contracts that you rely on to conduct business.

If you have entered into any agreement that provides service for your business, or ties you to a customer, you need to make sure that whoever wants to buy and to operate your business will be able to count on those same agreements. That may mean talking to your lawyer to determine the transferability of these understandings. And it may mean going to vendors or customers to make sure they'll accept the new owner of the business on the same terms they took you.

Agreements you've made with any of your employees should be handled the same way. Dealing with this issue can require the finesse of a career diplomat, but there are strategies for approaching the problem and you can ask your advisors – business broker or attorney – for advice. One solution, for example, is to take key employees into your confidence, let them known what is planned, and promise that once a successful sale is completed, they will be rewarded for keeping your secret and for their willingness to cooperate with a new owner.

I can't stress enough the importance of caution in the way this is handled, as this strategy backfired when I offered a business I was selling to a key employee. He immediately alerted the other employees about the impending sale, and this knowledge impacted operations. And not to the benefit of my business.

Licenses and permits

And don't forget the importance to the buyer of those clearances you've obtained from local, county and state governing bodies, over the years, to conduct your business and operate your equipment.

If you're the owner of any food business in California offering alcoholic beverages, you know your buyer will be required to apply for your ABC (Alcohol Beverage Control) license from an agency of the State. Ordinarily in the sale of such a business, the seller's license is transferred to the new owner after payment of a fee and application by the buyer, along with an investigation by the State.

Want to make sure the license transfer doesn't become a problem in your deal? Inform prospective buyers about what is required by the State at the earliest part of the introduction to the business. Provide the forms and let them know there'll be an investigation to learn where the purchase money came from, and to determine if any buyers have a business or personal connection with persons the State considers "undesirable".

If an eager buyer suddenly gets second thoughts when learning about this procedure, you'll be glad you were in a position to find that out. Now you can send the person on their way and spend your time with those buyers who are willing and able to make a deal.

And just because the business you want to sell is not ABC regulated, doesn't mean you escape the concern about government approval. If, for example, you use an air compressor, such as in an auto repair garage, or welding equipment of the type employed in, say, a machine shop, you'd better learn what local regulators require for your buyer to do, in order to operate the business with the same equipment.

There are a number of strategies that you and your buyer can employ to smooth the transition in cases where there are special approvals required. Whether it's the simple precaution of talking to the landlord beforehand, or a complicated tactic, such as using a corporate entity to work around a license transfer issue, the time to anticipate potential problems and deal killers and then work out solutions, is before, not after you've obtained a buyer.

Another bit of spade work you can do at this point, incidentally, has to do with lining up sources of cash the buyer can use to help with purchase price and working capital. Talk to business lenders, starting with your bank, to find out how much they can lend, what security they'll require (business assets or personal property or both) and what qualifications they will require of the buyer. Make sure your banker is aware that your business is running successfully and point out that the bank will likely be able to keep your business' account under a new owner, if it helps finance the deal. This pre-approval not only makes it easier for the buyer to work out the financing to complete the purchase, it also helps reinforce the value of the business in the buyer's mind. The business must be sound if the bank is prepared to make a loan to help with its purchase. The topic of financing a purchase will get more attention in a subsequent chapter, and is noted here to be added to your planning checklist.

It also is a solid idea for you to be prepared with the parts of the deal that you're to perform. Are you willing to train? For how long? During what hours? Does the buyer get your covenant not to compete? What are the terms, and how much of the value of the business do you place on the covenant? Also, how is the purchase price to be allocated? How much for goodwill? How will the tangible assets be valued?

Spring cleaning

This also is the best time – before offering your business for sale – to handle the unfinished business. Collect or write off your old receivables. If you're in the middle of a stalled legal dispute, try to get it resolved one way or another. If you're on notice to clean up a hazardous deposit or remove a public nuisance, there's no time like the present to make sure that matter is taken care of, once and for all. Even if you're not thrilled with what has to be done, it's worth doing now, rather than later. It'll free you up to deal with the next stage of your business life. And it will allow you to present your business free of difficulties and entanglements.

Do the Hard Work Now to Reap the Benefits Later

The smart seller knows that the best way to complete a deal, once an interested buyer is engaged, is to plan ahead to eliminate those nasty, deal killing surprises. California business brokers estimate that surprises account for nearly all of the 50% of agreements on small business sales that ultimately fall apart. And you can bet the surprises are rarely happy ones.

Yes, it's more work for you, but it's definitely in your best interests as a seller to find out what will be required for ownership transfer, and then do as much as possible to pave the way for the person who's interested in taking over the company – even before that person surfaces.

Conclusion

Sometimes the preparatory work reviewed in this chapter is the hardest part of selling. It may also be the difference between achieving, and failing to achieve, a satisfactory transaction to sell your small business in California.

KEY POINTS FROM THIS CHAPTER

❖ *Considering that purchase of a business is a critical, life-changing move for most buyers, and that their future financial well-being is in the balance, it isn't surprising that they are cautious and skeptical about the business opportunities they view.*

❖ *Your careful preparation when your business is offered for sale will substantially improve your chances of a deal at a fair and realistic price and terms. By contrast, lack of preparation is a major reason that 50% of accepted offers never make it through the due diligence examination to a closed escrow.*

❖ *"Once you start backpedaling, you're in trouble." This good advice is a reminder to make sure you have solid facts to support the statements about your business.*

❖ *Preparation of a business prospectus (also known as the offering package) with financials and assets lists, before the marketing effort begins, will allow you to respond promptly to interested buyers who need more information.*

❖ *Don't spend the first 30 to 60 days of your marketing campaign – the most critical time – trying to "get your act together." With all needed materials already assembled and in a package for qualified buyer prospects, you can turn your attention to the important responsibilities of interacting with buyers, responding to questions that are raised during the marketing, refining strategy and shaping your offering in response to market feedback, staying fully involved in the company to make sure its performance doesn't lag, and handling other tasks needed to sell your business.*

❖ *Can you get an appraisal or "statement of value" performed on your equipment? It helps to educate prospective buyers about what is being offered.*

❖ *Having your financial information audited is advisable for larger businesses (with selling prices above $500,000) and those with more complicated financial structures.*

❖ *The inclusion of "recast" financials with your P&L, helps the buyer understand how earnings might add up under his or her ownership.*

❖ Assemble and photocopy all written agreements important to the business, such as premises lease, advertising contracts and any customer, vendor or employee contracts so they can be provided to qualified buyer prospects.

❖ A two-page business profile giving a bit of the history and details of your operation is a useful addition to the business prospectus.

❖ A useful tool for putting together a business profile is a Business Profile form available on the internet at **www.bizben.com/selling-buying-business-forms.php**

❖ Including a description of the ideal buyer in the business prospectus helps to rule out unqualified buyers and save your time. It also might encourage those who qualify to further investigate your offering.

❖ Also include in the business prospectus an explanation of opportunities for growth and added profits that might await the new owner. Are there any newspaper or magazine articles that confirm your positive predictions by referring to the expansion in your industry or geographic area? If so, attach copies of these to your statement.

❖ Don't forget to include copies of marketing materials, ads, flyers, brochures and coupons in your business prospectus.

❖ Providing a serious buyer with a notice about problems you anticipate for the business, if any, helps to weed out those prospects for whom the problem is a deal killer. As the person would have discovered the negative information in due diligence, and then backed out of the deal, early disclosure of possible problems helps to prevent wasting time with the wrong buyers.

❖ Staging is the process of providing a level of information about the business that corresponds to a buyer's degree of interest. The first stage is a basic overview without identifying the company. Interim stages involve the disclosure of additional financial and other details to a buyer who is qualified and wants to further investigate the business. The final stage occurs after an agreement between buyer and seller for a transaction, subject to the buyer being satisfied with examination of all additional information. During this due diligence stage, the smart seller complies with most every reasonable request from the buyer for added details about the business.

❖ *A trial run is the seller's rehearsing the review of information that will be conducted by a buyer. The purpose is to make sure that all the material is clear, accurate and consistent, so there are no surprises when the buyer is engaged in the due diligence process.*

❖ *Assembling your professional team, including broker, attorney and accountant, is best done before the business is marketed. These professionals should understand their role, be familiar with what you are trying to accomplish and be prepared to assist. You might want to add to this group, an advertising specialist to help with parts of your business prospectus, such as the business profile.*

❖ *Details about terms of sale offered, including the allocation of purchase price, training agreement and seller's covenant not to compete should be worked out before the offering hits the market. In this way, the seller prevents the deal-delaying work that could have been handled earlier.*

❖ *Dealing with the landlord, franchisor, equipment leasing companies and others whose approval is needed to transfer assets of the business, should be done prior to offering the business for sale. Any problems should be resolved beforehand so that disruptions or surprises are eliminated or minimized.*

❖ *While it also might be a good idea to talk to key employees about the impending sale – in order to get their assistance, perhaps with an incentive for their discretion and cooperation – this plan should only be implemented if you're fairly certain the employee(s) can be trusted with the information.*

❖ *Preventing surprises and delays also means determining what licenses and permits need to be transferred and then, when possible, getting started on those processes.*

CHAPTER FOUR

BUYERS WANTED

After you've concluded that you're ready to sell your small California business, then determined specifically what it is you have to offer, and finally, finished pulling together the materials and information needed to complete the selling prospectus, you are almost at the point where you can start counting the proceeds from the sale.

Almost.

But first you need a buyer.

And there's some good news on this front. California is enjoying record sales of small businesses. The hot market is a consequence – in this, the middle of the first decade of the 21st Century – of the lackluster performance in the jobs market, driving many unemployed and underemployed workers to search out business opportunities for sale. If they can't get satisfactorily hired, many California workers dip into some of their home equity or retirement savings, or find some other source of funds so they can "buy" a career.

It is estimated by the business sales community that there are more buyers than ever searching for good deals in California right now. And they represent most every cultural, religious and ethnic group found in California's melting pot.

According to **www.bizben.com**, which operates an online database of small businesses for sale in California, at least 1,200 small businesses change hands in the state every month. And sometimes the monthly sold figure is as high as 2,900, with well over 4,000 small businesses on the market in California at any one time. For more information and complete statistics about sales of businesses in your area, go to **www.bizben.com/stats.php**

There's likely to be a buyer for most every small business, and for those businesses with a profitable past and a promising future, there are a number of buyers.

Think as if You're the Buyer

For you, the seller, it's useful to know who is out there in the buyer population and what they're looking for. And if you can put yourself in the shoes of the typical buyer, you'll gain valuable insight into how your offering is being viewed in the market.

If you've been observing the general business landscape, you've probably noticed the dynamics altering most every industry. Mid-sized companies are finding it harder to survive, as they compete both with the large, dominant players that are able to take the lion's share of business, and with the boutique-sized operations that are adept at quickly finding and exploiting niche markets in both consumer and business-to-business categories.

Does this trend apply in your case? To determine how you might capitalize on this phenomenon, just look at your business as it might be viewed by the two main types of buyers. You may be able to have your company acquired by an enterprise that's already a factor in your industry and is on a growth trajectory.

Alternatively, how about finding another independent operator who can continue, and perhaps build on, the small-business strategies you've found to be successful?

Get an Industry Insider to Acquire Your Business

If your livelihood comes from a small restaurant or grocery, or an operation that functions in the retail or service sectors, it may be difficult to find big players who are appropriate and interested buyers. But in some cases it's worth doing research to identify companies that might benefit if your customers and equipment became theirs.

Look for companies in your industry that are in a growth mode. In some cases, a competitor might be a logical buyer for your business.

One example of this is the vending industry, in which there is so much inbreeding – so many deals where one firm gobbles another – that it's not unusual for a route driver or office person to have worked for three different employers in a few years' time without once changing jobs. These moves often make a lot of economic sense. One company acquires machines and customers from another company for a price that's usually guided by a standard industry formula. The acquiring firm can add the business with little extra expense as new accounts are merely absorbed into the existing infrastructure. In other words, the beneficiary of the additional revenues can add much of that income directly to the bottom line. The office, the route system, many of the needed procedures and the know-how to run this new business already are in place. It's a classic example of efficiencies and profits resulting from the economies of scale.

And this principal works well in a number of industries, not just vending.

Is it possible one of the companies in your business – larger or not – could be your buyer? This approach has a number of advantages. Usually it's a quicker and easier deal with little likelihood of problems once the transaction has concluded. The acquiring firm may be a nearby organization that wants to expand local operations, or a geographic outsider interested in moving into your market. The buyer is probably quite familiar with your business, knows how to satisfy your customers and can use your resources to best advantage.

You'll find it unnecessary to educate an industry colleague about your business or answer endless questions about where customers come from and how to keep them coming back.

But the easier, cleaner deal may come at a price.

Right after your offering is presented for consideration to the managers of another company in your industry, they'll pull out their calculators and start performing computations. They'll use industry standard formulae to assign a value to your customers and your tangible assets. Then they'll run some return on investment analyses. Pretty soon, they'll arrive at a "right" price. That's the figure you'll be offered. Take it or leave it.

The buyer in this case, is comparing the cost of purchasing your company with a start-from-scratch scenario in which he sources the same assets you have and uses his experience to build up the business to an acceptable size in a certain period of time. That's usually a cheaper proposition, over the long run, than paying the asking price for your business.

If you want the maximum sales price for your small California business, this is usually not the best solution.

Additionally, there are sellers who shy away from opening their books to a competitor – someone who knows what they're looking at and might be able to use the information to the seller's detriment.

"What if these people don't buy the business after they find out where we source materials and inventory, and how we set our pricing? Why should we let them find out who some of our customers are?" That's a concern frequently voiced by sellers who wonder about the wisdom of showing details about their enterprise to someone else in the business.

Yes, it's standard procedure for prospective buyers – whether or not they compete with the subject business – to sign non-disclosure agreements before getting any sensitive information. But sellers often are – and probably should be – a bit skeptical about the degree of protection provided by these agreements.

In fact, attorneys who've studied these documents say the non-disclosure pledges don't really stop an unscrupulous competitor who plans to try gaining an unfair advantage with proprietary information about your business. To enforce such an agreement, you have to prove what the competitor did or is planning to do, that it is willful and calculated to achieve a result that violates the intent of the signed agreement. You also have to prove you are, or were damaged by the competitor's acts. Most business attorneys feel that's a tough assignment.

Another reason sellers balk at welcoming a competitor into the inner sanctum, is simply the automatic reaction that comes from having run up against the other company, taking their customers, having them lure away your salespeople, and just having gotten in the habit of considering them the enemy.

Looking for an Owner/Operator to Take Your Place

But there's another, perhaps more consequential reason many sellers prefer the more independent sectors of the business buying market. That's because most buyers from outside of the industry are willing – in the words of a CPA familiar with such transactions – "to pay a premium so they can gain access to the industry."

The buyer not affiliated with your industry – either a corporate refugee or someone planning to migrate from another business – typically looks at purchase price in a way that's more tolerant and less analytical than the buyer already schooled in the business. In fact, the market will tolerate more of what some brokers and agents call "blue sky" in the offering price of a business when it's targeted to buyers on the outside of the business.

Roughly 80 percent of likely prospects for small California businesses fit into this category of independent buyers – people who want to control their own working and career destinies rather than spend their productive years working for someone else and wondering if they could have done better in their own enterprise.

In the calculations of independent buyers, there is likely to be an emotional factor. This is in contrast to prospects in your industry who analyze offerings purely in terms of return-on-investment. If the independent buyer happens to like the way you earn your money, and can see himself or herself doing similar work, there will be less resistance to the notion of paying goodwill for the business. To some extent, the amount that a buyer is willing to pay above and beyond the value of hard assets, may relate to how much the buyer "feels a connection" with the mission or the day-to-day details of your enterprise.

An industry insider who has the ability to launch her own retail clothing business, but is considering buying yours, has both options available. If your asking price seems too steep, she can rent an empty store, fix it up, locate the merchandise she wants to sell and start from scratch.

But what about the person who wants to be in women's retail but hasn't the background to build from the ground up? She's probably smart to pay extra for an ongoing operation. The added cost, representing the value of an established business, will yield systems in place, customers already coming in the door and a seller to show her the ropes.

Similarly, a family looking at your dry cleaning plant as an opportunity to make a living is not comparing the offering to a cost analysis that involves starting a cleaning business from scratch. They don't want to take that risk. Instead, your small business offering is getting measured up against the stationery store, the quick print shop and the sandwich/coffee cart the buyers also have seen.

And since all of these operations are likely to be priced with a chunk of goodwill mixed in, prospective buyers are conditioned to the idea that paying extra just for the opportunity to get into their own business, simply comes with the territory.

So your best strategy, if you seek to maximize the selling price of your business, usually involves taking the time to introduce it to people not experienced in your business. Most sellers of small businesses in California do exactly that, focusing the marketing efforts on would-be owner/operators.

And that's where your buyer will most likely come from – an expanding category of entrepreneurs seeking business ownership, including disaffected corporate employees, people who have experienced (or who fear) the loss of their jobs, or individuals from other countries who've come to California seeking opportunities that may not be available to them at home.

But working with people who are inexperienced about business ownership is not without problems.

"These people ask the stupidest questions," one coffee shop owner complained to his broker. "If they can't tell the difference between cooking and warming something up in a microwave, how do they expect to be successful in this business?"

And if you think it's frustrating at the beginning of a sale to deal with buyers inexperienced in your business (some sellers regard it as "hand holding"), you should be aware that this is a mere annoyance compared to problems that can surface in the post-sale period.

More likely than not, the new owner of your business will lose some customers, or a key employee, or a valuable supply source. Stuff happens. And when the seller of a small company is no longer involved in the business relationships built over the years, even though she introduces the buyer to key people, there are likely to be some connections that vanish under the management of the new owner.

You can probably identify some individuals whose association with you is helpful to the business' success. If they were out of the picture you'd lose some profit, or you would have to work harder to replace what they brought to the business.

The smart seller and the careful broker and agent know the importance of explaining this principle to the incoming owner. And most buyers nod their heads in agreement when told that there are no guarantees, no promises that each and every customer will continue to do business, or that all the employees and vendors will maintain their loyal allegiance to the company.

Then, when the inevitable happens, some buyers roll up their shirtsleeves and get to work, soliciting new customers and learning the details of the business so they are not dependent on the employees inherited from the seller. Perhaps they'll call the seller and ask for a bit of advice.

But there are times when a sellers' contact from the buyer comes, not as a friendly business question, but in the form of a letter from a law firm explaining that the buyer's business problems are blamed on the poor condition in which the outgoing owner left the company. There may be an accusation that certain material information was not disclosed by the seller and broker. That's when sellers wonder if the deal with an inexperienced operator, even at a nice price, was such a good idea.

You can protect yourself with disclaimers. There even are methods of structuring a deal to anticipate a fall-off (or increase) in business during some of the post-sale period. This will be reviewed in a future chapter.

Even with intelligent precautions, however, there is a risk of post-sale problems and they're more likely to occur in your deal with an independent buyer.

Other Kinds of Buyers

By now, you might be getting an idea of what to expect when encountering prospective buyers for your small California business. Along with these pictures, it's helpful to remember that they are general rules and that there are many exceptions.

One exception is the buyer who comes from the ranks of your employees. This prospect is like an industry buyer, given his or her knowledge of your business, but is also like an independent buyer who will work in the business and rely on it as a major source of income.

Because of the concern noted in the last chapter about discussing, with employees, your interest in selling the business, this is a difficult kind of prospect to manage. The most successful strategy for selling to one employee or an employee group is probably to plan and prepare for it years in advance. There are MBO (Management BuyOut) and ESOP (Employee Stock Option Program) strategies which address the solid idea of employees taking over the company they work for when the owner retires or moves to another business. You'll need a financial professional to help you engineer such a plan. If he or she has enough time to develop a buyout strategy tailored to your business, a number of financing options can be used to make this successful.

Another exception of the basic two-kinds-of-buyer rule is the sale of a hobby type of business to an individual whose enjoyment of the subject of that business is greater than the concern about the cost of goodwill, or the rate of investment return. Your knitting shop or model railroad store might be a dream come true for a comfortably retired woman, or someone who wants to occupy his time, while the highly-paid spouse is at the office or on the road.

And in most every industry, there are financial buyers. These are, for the most part, investment bankers who set out to purchase several related businesses which they hope to combine under one corporate roof, boost profits by using economies of scale, and then resell the entire package at a substantial profit.

Although financial buyers are not particularly active in the range of businesses we're discussing – with selling prices under $5 million and most bringing under $1 million – you might encounter someone in this category who wants to look at your company. My experience is that a financial buyer represents the worst features of dealing with both the industry insider (lower price) and the owner operator (requiring your continuing involvement and a possible litigation risk).

But you should not rule out any potential purchaser for your business. If your offering is investigated by someone who plans to combine your business with others, for a later resale, you are well advised to hear them out, and look at what they are willing to do in order to take over your business.

Conclusion

Each of the two major kinds of buyers you are most likely to encounter, once you offer your company for sale, represents both advantages and disadvantages to the seller of a small California business. As you consider what you want for your business and how you want it sold, it is helpful to know what to expect from different kinds of buyers and determine which you want to work with.

KEY POINTS FROM THIS CHAPTER

❖ *The vigorous activity in small business sales in California is illustrated by the number of transactions every month – between 1,200 and 2,900.*

❖ *Information about small business sales in California can be accessed by visiting www.bizben.com/stats.php*

❖ *Some sellers want to work with other players in the same industry because a buyer like this will understand exactly what you have and will know how to incorporate your enterprise into their business. It means a minimum of work for you, because such a buyer will need little in the way of "hand-holding" or training from you.*

❖ *Inside-the-industry buyers are frequently able to work quickly because they have a short learning curve to determine if your business will be of value and because their approach to valuation is fairly standard.*

❖ *A number of sellers, perhaps you are included in this group, are unwilling to share proprietary information about their business with a competitor, and so this may not be an ideal choice for a possible buyer.*

❖ *The majority of buyers – some 80 % – for small businesses in California are individuals who are interested in – as articulated by a number of business brokers – "buying a job" or "buying a career." These are referred to as "outside" buyers or as "independent" buyers.*

❖ *Most sellers prefer to work with those who are interested in buying a company as a way of acquiring a new career. These independent buyers tend to pay the highest prices and that's why they dominate the market for small California businesses.*

❖ *There are drawbacks to the idea of selling to an independent buyer, including training requirements and the risk that the person will not be successful and will seek to blame you with a lawsuit.*

❖ *Variations on the idea of selling to industry insiders or to independent buyers include working with financial buyers who may buy your business if they can gain some value from it that you cannot, or hobbyists who purchase an enterprise aligned with their interests.*

❖ *A good buyer for your business, if you can plan way ahead, is an employee or group of employees. To pursue this strategy, you need a financial expert who can prepare a long-term buyout campaign in which, for example, part of the employee compensation is invested in a fund that will be used to purchase the business in the future*

CHAPTER FIVE

SHOULD YOU HIRE A BUSINESS BROKER TO HELP YOU SELL OR HANDLE IT YOURSELF?

Considering that hundreds – sometimes thousands – of small businesses are bought and sold in California every month, with many of these transactions requiring complicated structures and financing, it isn't surprising that there is an active community of business brokers and agents to service the needs of buyers and sellers. It's estimated that roughly one-third of the deals have at least one broker involved. Sometimes there are two representatives involved, providing service for both a buyer and a seller.

Licensed by the State of California under real estate law, business brokers and agents are required to know about the basics of contracts, negotiations, escrow, financing and related matters. And to be successful in this specialty, they should have a firm grounding in the disciplines of business accounting and of marketing.

The total of the two categories of licensees – brokers and agents – is about 900 people throughout the state. Most of them formally represent sellers, with a listing agreements serving as their agency contract. Most also work with buyers as a function of their responsibilities to selling clients. Some represent buyers only for a fee.

Brokers, Agents, Brokerages

A quick review here will help those readers who are unfamiliar with California brokerage law to understand the basic distinctions in discussing sellers' representatives.

A "broker" licensed by the state of California can conduct real estate, business opportunities transactions and related activities and supervise other licensees who do the same under the broker's license. Those supervised are usually "agents" who also are licensed, but under less stringent requirements compared to brokers. The broker is required to approve all agreements such as listings and sales contracts, in which he or she is involved, either as active participant or as supervisor, and has responsibilities for the legality and proper execution of such agreements. Brokers can be liable for illegal, improper or unethical practices conducted in the execution of the broker's business.

Agents also can be liable if their practices violate California law or code of ethics.

"Brokerage" is a company established to provide services in the real estate, business opportunities and related markets. Every brokerage is required to have a licensed broker as an employee, owner or officer.

It might also be noted that a licensed California attorney is authorized to perform many of the duties of a broker.

The term broker in this discussion means the legal representative of the seller – either a broker or an agent working under the supervision of a broker, with whom the seller has most contact.

The Choice

As owner of a small California business with an interest in selling, one of the many choices you need to make is whether you'd like to be represented by a licensed broker or simply handle the whole matter yourself, perhaps with assistance from your accountant, attorney and other advisors. Do you want to tap into the resource of California business brokers or is this something you feel you can manage on your own?

The independent, self-sufficient spirit which drives some entrepreneurs into business ownership may cause them to rule out the idea of relying on anyone else when it comes time to sell. If you are one of these people you may feel that no one can represent you as well as you can manage the job yourself. You may fear that your time will be wasted with unqualified buyers brought by overeager representatives. And you worry that the information about your business, and the fact that it is for sale, won't be treated confidentially. And you do want to make sure, for business reasons, that employees and customers are not aware of your attempts to find a new owner.

If you are a do-it-yourself kind of seller, you may benefit by becoming familiar with the steps involved in the marketing and sale of a business, as described in the paragraphs that follow. Even if you are planning to work with a broker, or you're still undecided on this matter, you'll find it helpful to review these concepts so that you are informed about what needs to be done in order to achieve a satisfactory sale.

The Business Sales Process

Review the two dozen services that you can expect from a business broker or agent. Then ask yourself if you're able and willing to perform all these functions on a do-it-yourself basis:

- Provide advice and assistance in preparing the business for sale. The representative might act something like a personal coach in helping and encouraging you to carry out the preparation assignments noted in an earlier chapter.

- Furnish market intelligence, which can be very valuable when determining how to package and present your business in a way that insures a welcome reception when it goes on the market.

- Offer experienced counsel in establishing an asking price high enough for you to get a maximum value from your sale, but not so high that it discourages interest in your offering.

- Aid in structuring your business offer so that it's attractive to a purchaser without derailing your tax plan, or otherwise harming your interests.

- Suggest ways to find financing so as to increase the appeal and marketability of your business. Some of these financing techniques can be built into the structure of your offering.

- Create a marketing plan and produce the materials that will be used to offer your business for sale. This requires a special set of skills borrowed from the world of advertising.

- Expose the business offering to a current and active database of pre-qualified buyers. Sometimes this procedure can successfully result in a sale in a few days.

- Promote your business for sale in an intelligent and aggressive manner to a general population of buyers so your offering receives wide, controlled exposure. The "controlled" aspect is designed to satisfy your concerns about confidentiality. A variety of promotion outlets may be used, including **www.bizben.com**

- Enlist a network of business brokers and agents to aid in finding a buyer, using informal systems as well as more formal measures, such as an interbroker business listing service.

- Gather and analyze market feedback and use it to adjust the structure of your offering if that will improve marketability. A great deal of experience, sound judgment and creativity are needed in this process.

- Contribute experience and know-how to help in the difficult task of maintaining confidentiality.

- Interview buyer candidates to make sure they are qualified and have agreed in writing to your requests regarding confidentiality. Eliminate those candidates who don't meet the criteria.

- Introduce qualified, interested buyers to your business.

- Conduct follow-up with prospective buyers to determine who is truly interested in your offering.

- Solicit offers for your business – a job that requires a range of skills as will be discussed in a later chapter.

- Utilize creative persistence and patience for the challenging task of orchestrating negotiations.

- Manage the due diligence process to make sure it is quickly and satisfactorily completed.

- Help to answer questions and resolve issues that surface during the escrow period.

- Contribute the energy and skillful diplomacy sometimes required to keep the escrow moving forward through difficulties and over obstacles.

- Provide the seller with ongoing consultation, advice and reassurance throughout the difficult periods in a sale.

- Maintain a marketing effort so there are back-up offers. This important process allows a seller to have alternatives if the buyer does not perform, and keeps the buyer motivated to complete the purchase.

- Use experience and knowledge to make sure seller is not unnecessarily exposed to the many risks that can be inherent in a business transaction.

- Supervise the close of escrow to make sure everything is done correctly and seller's interests are protected.

- Help seller with any post-sale matters.

Benefits of Doing These Yourself

Suppose you have read and thought about this list of the two dozen responsibilities of a business broker or agent toward a seller client, and it sounds like a job description for you.

As noted above, there are a number of reasons some sellers prefer to self-represent. There are those who feel no one can do a job as well as they can. Then there are sellers so worried about a possible breach of confidence that they want to be involved every time someone is told about their offering.

However, the three most frequently cited reasons for a seller to reject the assistance of the business brokerage community are: the fee, the fee and the fee.

And it is not surprising that a business owner who's had to watch every penny in order to be successful thinks twice, and three times, about engaging the services of a representative in the sale of the business. It means giving up a chunk of the sales proceeds, usually in the range of 10% to 12% of the final selling price.

Some sellers think they can get a bargain by listing with a broker who's accustomed to real estate transactions but wants to try selling a business. The bargain part of it comes about if the broker charges the standard commission – 6% of the selling price – used in home sales. My experience is that sellers trying to save money this way will most likely learn that "you get what you pay for." And that's in the best case! You'll learn more about this in the next chapter.

And the Disadvantages of Being Your Own Broker

This job is not for you, however, if you don't feel you have the skills – or the time – to act as your own representative and run your business too.

Besides, you may not be well-served if you attempt to perform the function of a dispassionate third-party. You have a substantial personal stake in the outcome of this campaign. It will be difficult for you to maintain the objectivity needed in all phases of the process of selling your business. That applies especially when you get to the part where the price and terms are being hammered out.

Benefits of Engaging a Broker

Using a third party is also beneficial in cases where there are deficiencies in your offering, but because it is your business, no one wants to volunteer their criticism or advice. They don't want to hurt your feelings. A disinterested representative is much more likely than you are to learn how your business offering is received by the market. And what your representative finds out can be vital intelligence that you need in order to ultimately find a qualified buyer and close a deal.

If you are in a quandary as to whether you want to engage the services of a representative – you don't want to do the work, but you also don't want to give up a commission – you should know that a professional in the business opportunities field is likely to get a higher price for your business than you will. That's because he or she will be in touch with many more buyers than you. The more prospective purchasers for your business, the greater the chance of getting the requested price. Besides, many brokers and agents have exceptional selling skills they can use to determine the top dollar likely to be paid for your business, and then persuade an interested buyer to agree to that figure.

And, just as your experience in your business has taught you to anticipate and prevent problems, and find solutions when the problems aren't prevented, seasoned business brokers and agents can come to the rescue if you encounter difficulties in the sale of your business that you don't know how to solve. In many cases brokers are able to put things back on track when it appears a deal is headed for failure.

One frequent problem that most skilled brokers can deal with is the buyers' remorse or second thoughts issue that afflicts a number of transactions if they drag on slowly, over a period of several weeks. Brokers are familiar with the pace of a healthy deal and usually are able to keep that pace going, even when questions or problems appear during negotiations, or while parties are engaged in the due diligence process.

Something else to think about, if you're debating benefits vs. costs of engaging a representative to help sell your small California business, is the matter of your protection. Even the most experienced business people can be vulnerable to the risk of getting entangled with one of the many difficult situations that can ruin a sale, disrupt the marketing of your business or expose you to unnecessary liabilities. A skilled business broker knows what to watch out for, and can usually steer you clear of legal and other hazards as the business is placed on the market and taken through the complete cycle to a closed escrow.

Is it Worth the Fee?

If you interview a few business brokers and agents, you'll learn that their fees are usually a percentage of your selling price, typically between 10 and 12. There may be a minimum fee for transactions with low selling prices. And if the size of your business warrants a price in excess of $1 million, a business broker may determine the commission using a formula with a sliding scale tied to final selling price.

Only you can decide if it is worth the fee to have a representative help you in the sale. Be sure to consider all the factors – the time and skill required, the risks involved, the possibility that a business broker will be able to sell for a higher price – as you do the cost/benefit analysis.

Hybrid Agreements

What if you have a buyer, someone who is already interested in owning your business, and you'd like some help putting the deal together? Or suppose you currently have the business listed and you are approached by a buyer, independently of your representative. And how should you handle this situation: A buyer is introduced during a listing, the listing expires and the buyer returns without the broker, wanting to deal with you individually – suggesting that since the broker is no longer involved, the price can be lower? And is there a way to get two different brokers working for you if you like them both and don't want to choose one to the exclusion of the other?

These and a number of other, similarly perplexing situations are rather common occurrences in the market for small businesses in California. You, a seller, should be aware of different arrangements with brokers and agents that can help deal with these scenarios.

The listing agreement

For starters, it would be useful to review the basic characteristics of a listing agreement – the employment contract that a broker and a seller each sign to define their relationship. Just like a listing agreement on a house, this is the promise of the broker to market the subject property – in this case a business opportunity – for sale, to show and provide information about the property for the benefit of prospective buyers, to solicit offers, aid in negotiations between buyer and seller, and work to secure a ratified transaction (a deal that's signed by both buyer and seller). The cost of this work, including advertising fees and incidental expenses, is paid by the broker. In return for this promise, the seller pledges to pay the broker a commission. The commission amount is always specified in the agreement and usually is expressed as a percentage of the selling price. The commission, also called the fee, is customarily due to be paid upon the broker's successful accomplishment of his or her tasks, when the work culminates in a sale.

The base agreement is called an Exclusive Right to Sell. It commences on the date specified in the contract and terminates at an agreed date in the future – usually three or six months from the beginning date, sometimes longer.

In fact you may be asked to sign a listing for a full year or more. It is my experience that you're better served by an agreement that keeps your broker working on your behalf. Consequently, I feel a six month listing is the maximum period to which you should agree. If the broker is doing a good job of representing you and is working hard to sell your business, but there still is no sale after the end of the listing period, you can simply agree to an extension of the listing contract for another three or six months.

Because of the provision about exclusivity in this type of listing, the brokerage in the contract is the only one authorized to represent the seller in this capacity during the life of the agreement and any extensions. And the broker is entitled to a commission if the subject property is sold to anyone during the listing period, whether that buyer is obtained by the broker or not. The agreements almost always specify that if a buyer, introduced to the property while the listing is active, comes back later, after the listing's expiration, the broker is entitled to the commission if a sale to that buyer is achieved within a specified period of time after the introduction took place. For example, if a buyer is introduced by the business broker to a service station in May, and waits till after September (four months later) when the listing expires, to make an offer to purchase the station, the broker still is entitled to a commission if a deal is struck between buyer and seller. This is meant to protect the broker's right to commission if a seller and buyer want to have a deal, and collude to save the commission by postponing their buy/sell contract till after the listing expires.

As you might imagine, it's important for brokers and sellers to keep track of whom they talked to, and when. If there is a dispute under a listing contract the final determination of rights will probably hinge on the facts of the case. And parties involved will need to prove their version of what happened.

As the Exclusive Right to Sell contract provides brokers the most control and protection it is the form of agreement used for the majority of listings. And it is the one recommended by most brokers and agents.

But there are other kinds of agreements by which brokers and sellers contract to do business. You should be aware of your options. And you also should be aware that many brokers and agents decline to enter into a hybrid listing.

Exclusive Agency

If you select a single broker to represent you, but want the right to sell to your own buyer without an obligation to the broker for a commission, the most appropriate agreement is Exclusive Agency. You are not permitted to sign with other brokers, according to this understanding. For you to make the sale without obligation to the broker, remember that you must be able to demonstrate that the buyer is someone you contacted independently, not a person introduced to the business by the broker.

Open listing

Under this looser arrangement the broker is assured of being compensated for a sales commission if, and only if, that broker comes up with the ultimate buyer. It is like a finders' agreement. Meanwhile, the seller is free to make his or her own sale and to work with most any other broker without obligation to anyone except the broker who introduced the buyer under an Open listing.

One Party listing

A variation on the Open listing, the One Party agreement can be used when the seller is not willing to offer the business for sale through the broker in the usual way, but is willing to pay a specified commission to a broker if the one person mentioned by name on the One Party listing purchases the business.

This kind of agreement might come about in the case where a broker approaches a business owner and explains that he has a client interested in purchasing the business. The broker may say he wants to introduce that individual to the business, handle any resulting transaction and receive a commission for a successful sale. In the event the owner's response is: "If this person buys the business for my price, I'll pay you the commission," the result can be a One Party listing between seller and broker, naming that buyer, and specifying the price and terms requested by the seller. If a seller agrees to a listing like this, it's a good idea to include an expiration date.

Should You Pay a Fee Upfront?

Though not a listing, there is a form of agreement used by some in the industry in California who require a fee before any work is done to aid the seller of a small business. In my experience most sellers who've agreed to this arrangement regret it later on, as they seldom get any value for the money they pay.

Sellers are well advised to refrain from entering into any agreements calling for an up-front payment, unless there will be a valuable service – such as advertising or a business appraisal by an established valuation expert – provided in return.

Conclusion

Sellers learning about various types of listings and then expecting to make special arrangements to get a business broker's services without granting exclusivity, should be advised that many brokers are not willing to depart from the basics of the exclusive representation agreement.

Some competent brokers are willing to work on the basis of the different forms of representation. But the seller who wants the most attention, support and services from a representative in the brokerage community will usually have to give the broker full control and commission rights for any deal that is made, or involving any interested buyer obtained, during the listing period.

When deciding whether or not to represent yourself in the sale of your business, it's helpful to know the 24 important jobs that need to be performed and determine if you are prepared to handle them. It also helps to consider the risks involved when sellers handle their own business transaction.

KEY POINTS FROM THIS CHAPTER

❖ *Sellers have a choice of representing themselves or contracting with a licensed representative to help find a buyer and achieve a satisfactory transaction.*

❖ *Those licensed by California to provide services to business owners wanting to sell are brokers and agents. Brokers must satisfy more stringent licensing requirements than agents. And brokers are legally responsible not only for their own conduct but also for that of the agents in their employee. Agents also are responsible for their conduct.*

❖ *Some 24 separate and important functions are performed by brokers when assisting their clients to sell a business.*

❖ *Entrepreneurial type business owners may be more inclined to represent themselves in the marketing and sale of their businesses. They should keep in mind all of the costs and risks involved.*

❖ *There are a number of different arrangements that a seller can make with a broker for representation.*

❖ *Hybrid listing agreements include the Exclusive Agency (you have the right to sell the business yourself but can only work with one broker), the Open listing (allowing you to sell the business yourself with no obligation to anyone, and to work with as many brokers as you want, paying only the broker who is successful), the One Party listing (which allows a broker to introduce your business to the party named and specifies the commission the broker will receive if that party becomes your buyer.)*

❖ *The disadvantage of entering into a hybrid agreement with a broker for sale of your business is that you may not get the same degree of careful and aggressive service from someone who doesn't have complete exclusivity in their listing contract for your company.*

❖ *Sellers are well advised not to enter into agreements that call for fees "up front" unless there is a valuable service provided in return, such as advertising the business for sale – in which event the fee should be related to actual advertising costs – or conducting an expert valuation of the business.*

CHAPTER SIX

HOW TO SELECT AND WORK WITH A BUSINESS BROKER

Although they may not have as much formal education as professionals in the medical, the legal and some aspects of the financial services industry, business brokers can be just as vital to your well-being, certainly your financial health, as the more traditionally respected advisors.

And just as it would be a mistake to take your nagging medical condition, or a difficult legal problem to a professional with a low level of competence, you definitely want to avoid business brokers who lack the know-how and resources to provide you the services needed to successfully sell your small California business at the right price and terms.

Many business brokers – as is true of professionals in other fields – are committed to giving consistent, quality service to clients. Of the 900 or so people working in California as brokers or agents on small business transactions, the majority make every effort to be honest and ethical in their dealings. They continue to learn about their field so as to be on top of changes and new developments, and their dedication and hard work is a positive reflection on their industry.

And, as in other fields, there are a few business brokers who do not adhere to high standards of ethics and performance.

Improve Your Odds of Selling with an Able Business Broker

Choosing correctly between a competent professional and the hack – who may talk a good game but can't deliver – is important for someone contemplating the sale of a small business. Imagine the consequences of working much of your career to build a successful enterprise, cherishing the dream of having it provide for your later, post retirement years, then choosing the wrong business broker to manage that critical process. It's a horror story that happens more often than it should in California.

In many cases a business owner has one good shot at selling. Blow that opportunity and there may not be others.

It was pointed out earlier that selling a business is unlike selling a house or a piece of income property. A poorly handled job of real estate marketing, may cause a delay in completing a sale. After a ruined deal, a new buyer has to be found and the process begins again. In most cases, the home or real estate investment retains its value and marketability, even though it was originally presented improperly, or matched with an unqualified buyer, or subjected to other errors that can cause a deal to fall apart.

But a business – whether a liquor store, restaurant or tree trimming service – that sits on the market too long, can easily acquire a bad reputation, a negative stigma that hangs on like a summer cold. The word gets out that something must be wrong because no one has stepped up to buy it after several weeks or months of trying. Employees get nervous and may leave. And even some regular customers, if they hear rumors about what's happening, are likely to start patronizing other companies. Indeed, the value and the marketability of a business can easily be damaged by an unsuccessful campaign to sell it.

The selling effort, to be successful, should start strong, with all marketing materials, business information and important documents in place. An able broker will help orchestrate the introduction of your offering to the world of buyers, knowing that the first 30 to 60 days of marketing a business can be the most critical. Even if yours is a clean and profitable business, the market for it can be difficult to explore because of the natural skepticism of buyers and the abundance of business offerings they have to analyze – so many of which are not viable.

An offering not really prepared to be shown, or not aggressively marketed in this difficult environment, can take more than a year to get matched with a ready, willing and able buyer – that is, if it is does not become one of the majority (70% of small California businesses) which never get sold although the efforts are made. By contrast, successful brokers know that they frequently can look forward to a deal in one to six months when offering a listing that is completely readied for sale and correctly promoted.

As noted in the previous chapter, there are a number of critical steps involved in the process of a sale. In searching for a broker, you want to find someone who can manage these steps effectively, so that you, the seller, get to collect your money and turn over the key to a new owner. Your challenge will require the skilled work of a professional who knows how to recognize and deal with the many potential problems that could cause your sale to fall apart.

There's no reason you can't interview three or four, even more prospective brokers to find the one you feel can best help sell your business. You'll find some of the most active business brokers in you're area at **www.bizben.com**.

Specific Characteristics to Look For

Here are some guidelines to help you make an intelligent and informed choice.

Experience

Business brokers are familiar with this story, or one like it, and enjoy telling it because it seems humorous in contrast with the real world of business sales: The owner of a window treatment service learned that his brother-in-law had just received a real estate license and had joined a brokerage with the intent of selling businesses. As the company owner wanted to retire, he visited the brother-in-law's office with one of his employees, a man who wanted to purchase the firm. They'd already worked out a price and terms, had talked to the landlord about transferring the lease on the warehouse, and had visited City Hall to obtain the forms they needed to fill out, so as to transfer all permits and licenses required to operate the business.

"We want you to write up the deal," the seller told his relative.

With a bit of help from the office manager, the brother-in-law completed the buy/sell agreement and the supporting documentation, then arranged for buyer and seller to visit a business escrow service frequently used by the brokerage.

After the obligatory waiting period following publication of the bulk transfer notice, the buyer and seller signed the final documents, the money was dispersed and everyone shook hands on the deal.

"Boy," said the brother-in-law, returning to his office and handing the commission check from escrow to his manger, "this is a great business."

If every deal went like that you'd be safe selecting most any business broker, even one who lacked a track record of closing deals. But that example is an exception – a rare exception – to the customary circumstances involving business transactions.

What's normal is this: Even if the sale of your business goes relatively smoothly, you can anticipate a wait of several days to several months before a qualified and suitable buyer is found. You can expect disagreements throughout the negotiating process. Your needs and requests will often differ from those of the buyer.

And once a deal is achieved, you can almost surely count on unexpected circumstances threatening to delay, or even sabotage your transaction.

This is no place for an amateur!

What if the landlord is uncooperative? Suppose the escrow receives requests from a vendor or customer, claiming there are unresolved disputes with your company, and asking for a portion of the sellers' proceeds – your money – to be paid out to the claimant at close. Imagine the difficulties if a government agency contacts escrow and enters a claim for unpaid fees or taxes. Even though the claim is in error, it may needlessly spook the buyer.

These are common occurrences in a "normal" business transaction and why half the contracted deals for small businesses in California never make it to close of escrow.

Steering among these obstacles takes the cool head and steady hand of someone who's dealt successfully with these problems. And even if your sale is threatened by a set of circumstances your broker has never before observed, the knowledge and judgment she's formed over her years of working with similar issues should prepare her to deal quickly with the new challenges.

Look for a business broker who has chalked up at least two years of full time work, actively listing, selling and closing deals.

You may be impressed by the energy of someone new to the industry. There's no doubt that a beginner's enthusiasm is valuable for a difficult project, such as selling a business. It's reassuring to have a representative we feel will work extra hard on our behalf just to prove himself. But before you turn your business over to an unseasoned representative, make sure the person has plenty of support back at the office so that you can benefit from the experience gained by your business broker's colleagues.

Knowledge

Closely linked with the importance of experience, is the requirement that your broker is knowledgeable about every aspect of business sales. Knowing the law is vital. So is intimate familiarity with the procedures to be followed from the moment a contract is signed to the closing of escrow.

A Northern California business escrow officer, who likes to emphasize the importance of knowing the rules, tells the story of a broker who opened an escrow for sale of a dairy route and was surprised, days later, to learn why the buyer wasn't returning his calls or cooperating with the escrow.

It turns out the buyer had found another business that he wanted more, even after learning the dairy route seller had accepted his offer. And because the buyer never acknowledged, in writing, the acceptance of his offer for the dairy route, there was no contract. It was a technicality, but it allowed the buyer to squirm out of the agreement, leaving seller and broker without the deal they thought they had.

The moral of this story is that the broker's lack of knowledge about contract law resulted in a problem for both the broker and for the seller.

It's not your job as the seller to know the ins and outs of business sales requirements in California. But you should inform any brokers who want your business that it's important they know the rules and are consistent in applying them. Anyone who isn't fully informed about California law regarding business sales, or who isn't careful to follow the law, should not be selected to represent you.

References

But how does the seller know, for sure, the depth of experience or extent of knowledge possessed by a candidate for the job of his or her business broker?

That's why it's vital to get a list of sellers, at least five – ten is better, for whom the broker has worked.

Ask for names and contact information.

Then be sure to call or email every one of them. Don't stop at the two who head the list. Anyone can find two people to brag about his honesty and business expertise. Communicate with every reference, ask if there were problems with their deals and whether the broker was able to handle those difficulties. Was the broker easy to work with? Was he or she able to keep the transaction moving toward completion, or did it stall because of unanticipated complications, misunderstandings and uncompleted tasks? Did the broker convey an attitude of competence? Were there any post-sale complaints?

Ask the contact whether any stumbling blocks or delays in their transaction were the result of broker inattention. And ask if the person would hire that same broker again, and whether they'd recommend that others do the same.

And be sure to find out when the reference and the broker were involved together in a business transaction. The more recent the better. I'm usually leery of references that are more than three or four years old.

Most people feel that the willingness to submit a list of references is somehow proof of ability. "Surely she wouldn't give me these references if they aren't good," the reasoning goes.

But brokers have been known to provide a list of people in response to the request and then hope and assume – in many cases correctly – that the references will never be contacted.

If, in checking your prospective brokers list of references, you find his gardener, his next door neighbor, and a couple of business owners who never had success working with him, it's best to assume that the broker never expected you to actually contact the names on the list. You can also conclude that the broker does not qualify to handle your business.

Resources

Talent, experience and knowledge are key attributes to look for in the broker who will help you successfully sell your business. And these abilities should be grounded with the resources that enable brokers to access buyers, generate wide promotion of your offering and locate the services – such as lending and escrow support – that will make it possible for you to realize your goal of selling your business.

Is the prospective broker a member of a multiple listing network? Does he/she use online services such as **www.bizben** to make sure a listing receives the widest exposure possible? Where does the broker's buyer prospects come from? Are they pre-qualified?

Find out if the prospective representative has relationships with escrow companies, business appraisers, equipment valuation services, inventory services and small business lenders. You'd like to learn, when interviewing prospective brokers, not only what they know, but also who they know and on whom they can call to help in the campaign to make you a happy "former" small business owner.

Rapport

Think of your business broker as a member of your team. And consider that accomplishing most anything is easier with teamwork.

Certainly that's true in the case of a project as difficult as finding a buyer for a small California business, helping that person through his or her examination of the business, negotiating an agreement acceptable to all parties, getting the permits and approvals necessary to complete the transition, then handling all final details so the deal can be successfully closed.

To get your business sold in a reasonable period of time at the price and terms you want, may not require that you and your broker work together with the precision of a super bowl-winning quarterback and his favorite receiver. Or a brain surgeon and chief surgical assistant. But if there's poor communication and a lack of understanding between the two of you, the task will be much more difficult, if not impossible.

It's critical that your broker clearly understands your needs and priorities and it's important that you know what to realistically expect your broker to be able to do. In the heat of negotiations, or during the difficult periods of due diligence, it's easy to let emotion influence reason. Even the calmest, most logical sellers can find themselves frustrated when things don't move according to plan. That's when it's particularly important that you and your broker have a person-to-person connection that allows you to work through tough problems so you can achieve your final goal.

But you can't approach this need with objective solutions, as you would when asking a broker-candidate about years of experience, and requesting a list of references. The question of rapport needs to be answered by you, using more subjective analysis.

Are you able to communicate with this person? Does he or she understand your problems? Does the broker candidate clearly express himself or herself about the challenges you will face and do you get the impression the person is prepared for those challenges?

These are some of the more subtle of the factors that go into choosing a business broker to work with. They're not easy to quantify or describe objectively. And yet, how you "feel" about your business broker can greatly influence your ability to work together. It's also a predictor of your likelihood for success.

Honesty and trust

One of the failings of small business sellers, particularly those who never get to experience the success of a completed deal, is the powerful desire to hear good news. That's true for virtually all humans – that we want to receive confirmation of our own beliefs. We love to learn that things are going well, that the outcome we want for a situation is close at hand.

But when you are interviewing business brokers, keep in mind how essential it is that you are made aware of all of the relevant facts – whether or not you want to hear them – whenever it's necessary for you to make a decision.

Sellers do well to avoid brokers who seem to be embellishing or exaggerating when they talk about their accomplishments or predict what they can do. In their eagerness for business they may be setting the stage for big trouble to follow.

Imagine what can happen if the "rosy picture" conveyed to a buyer by this broker is deemed to be a misrepresentation of the facts. That can bring serious consequences not only for the broker, but also for a client – and that's you.

Maybe it's acceptable to "stretch the truth" when describing the fish you almost caught last weekend, but there is absolutely no place for anything but the cold hard facts when it comes to the business of selling businesses.

Some of the questions that may help you separate the truth-tellers from those prone to exaggerate are: What's the right price to sell my business? How long will it be before I get a deal? Can I get all cash for my business?

If your broker candidate tells it "like it is," you may not enjoy hearing all of the answers. A realistic assessment about price and terms, and the length of time it will take to close a deal, might not correspond with what you had hoped for. But you'll do well to select a broker who tells you the facts. It means you'll save valuable time and you'll know where you stand throughout the process.

"I think a seller should experience as much of their disappointment as possible before they actually go to the market," says one business broker. "That way, we find out right at the beginning if they can't deal with the truth."

"Once we have the unrealistic expectations out of the way, we can start doing business in the real world. And that's how you get your business sold."

How to Work With Your Business Broker

Assuming you've selected an experienced, knowledgeable and entirely honest broker with substantial selling resources and with whom you have a great rapport, it's imperative that you work effectively with this person to achieve your objective.

One colleague tells the story of a woman who engaged the services of a business broker specifically known for his experience in the beauty services industry so she could sell her hair salon and retire. Although the seller found it a bit difficult to deal with him, she was impressed with the glowing recommendations from the referrals she checked and with his experience. In fact, the broker came to the salon a day after the listing was taken, bringing a buyer who owned other, similar, businesses.

The prospective buyer proceeded to fire off a series of questions that the seller was unable to answer. Curiously, he didn't care to learn about her customers, the equipment, or the other dynamics that the seller considered important to the business. This buyer was apparently interested only in the financials. And the things he was investigating – "dollars per chair" and "profit per employee" – were principles she hadn't studied, though she'd run the shop successfully for over 20 years.

Not only did the seller not see that buyer again, she didn't hear much from the broker after that. She eventually learned that the broker considered her "difficult to deal with," apparently because she didn't have the kinds of analyses at her finger tips, that he required.

After expiration of the six month listing with that broker, the seller again interviewed brokers, this time choosing a less experienced professional, but one with whom she could easily communicate. Eventually the business was sold, but it took longer than the seller had anticipated.

The story points out the importance of a good understanding between seller and broker, and the fact that the seller didn't do a very good job of learning what would be required of her. She didn't insist on feedback from the marketing campaign, and she failed to push her representative to make a real sales effort on behalf of her business. The broker was at fault as well. But it was the seller who suffered the impact of their poor relationship and she realized later, when talking to the new broker, that she should have been more proactive with the original representative.

To work effectively with your broker, it is imperative that you can communicate with one another. Make sure the professional representing you will be in touch with you at least two or three times a week. In fact, you can have that provision written right into the listing agreement.

Have the broker put in writing how frequently you can expect to receive an update on the marketing efforts – who has been introduced to your business, what the reaction was and so forth. You even can ask that the broker specify the dollar figure that will be spent to promote and advertise your business for sale. (A budget of $2,000 or so is not unreasonable). Covering these points in the listing agreement helps to set the tone for the seller/broker relationship. And if there is a good relationship, with plenty of communication and realistic expectations on both sides, you stand a better chance of accomplishing the sale of your business at a satisfactory price and terms.

It's not critical that the broker specializes in your type of business, but it is important that he or she is willing to work hard to make sure your business is exposed to many potential buyers. And while some sellers are impressed if a representative brags about having a large "stable" of listings – as if every business person in town wants their help – I think you're better off dealing with someone who has a half dozen listings. With a manageable inventory, your broker will have the time to give you the service your business needs, so it can be marketed properly and sold in a reasonable period of time.

As noted in the prior chapter, you should avoid so-called "listings" that require a fee to be paid at the beginning. If there is no value provided, except for the broker's claim that he or she will do their best to find you a buyer, you'll soon meet with a big disappointment – perhaps an expensive one. If you're going to pay for services, make sure you receive something you can use, such as a package that promotes your business in an appealing way, or an appraisal conducted by a trained small business valuation expert to establish what your business is worth.

It's fair to ask a prospective broker to limit the length of your exclusive agreement to three months or six months. If you feel the person and their brokerage are doing a good job for you, but the listing expires before a sale is achieved, you can always agree to an extension. This puts you in a stronger position and is preferable to getting locked into a longer Exclusive Right contract (such as nine-month or 12-month listing) with someone who feels they have plenty of time and doesn't quite get around to selling your business.

It is not fair, however, to keep important information from your broker. Your business is not expected to be perfect. It may have deficiencies in, for example, the length of the lease, the dependence on a small number of major customers, or the deteriorating condition of your equipment. It's important that you level with the professionals representing you. Don't surprise them. Let them help you by disclosing to them all of the aspects of your offering that may be a problem in finding a buyer.

Keeping secrets from, and springing unexpected facts on your broker merely interrupts the selling momentum and disrupts your relationship. And those are the kinds of problems that interfere with a successful sale of your business.

Conclusion

Small business owners – ordinarily able to exhibit sound judgment – may suddenly become less rational, even forget to use their critical thinking skills, when considering the sale of their business. Perhaps it's wishful thinking overcoming their good sense. Maybe they're overwhelmed by the idea of selling, or intimidated by the process.

The choice of the professional needed to help sell your business should be made in much the same way that you select a doctor or lawyer. Look for people with experience and knowledge of their field. Seek a representative whom you trust, and with whom you can communicate. And by all means, obtain and check those references.

Then, once you've selected a professional to help you sell, work with that person. Give your broker all of the pertinent facts about your offering – the bad news as well as the good – and make sure you do your part to maintain open and honest communication throughout the process.

KEY POINTS FROM THIS CHAPTER

❖ *In many cases a small business owner in California has one good shot at selling. Make sure, if you engage a broker to represent you, that he or she is fully qualified and totally committed to helping you succeed.*

❖ *Unlike real estate, a small California business that is poorly marketed may suffer a decline in value and desirability. The negative impact is a consequence of over-exposure and the risk of lost business.*

❖ *The first 30 to 60 days that a small business is offered for sale in California can be the most critical period in its marketing cycle. If the offering is not fully prepared and aggressively promoted by the listing broker right from the start, the interest in it may decline, with a resulting drop off in saleability.*

❖ *Small businesses in California that are properly prepared and correctly promoted have a good chance of getting sold in one to six months. Those that are less effectively handled might remain on the market up to 18 months, before being sold. And these two categories cover just the 30% of small California businesses that eventually are purchased. Some 70% of offerings are never matched with a buyer.*

❖ *Look for characteristics in a prospective broker that are associated with success in selling small California businesses on the seller's terms. These include experience (at least two years working full-time in business brokerage), knowledge (of the law, of proper procedure and of solutions to problems), and ample resources (of buyers and other brokers who might have buyers).*

❖ *Asking the hard questions about the proper price and selling terms for your small California business may help you determine who, among prospective brokers, will give you the information you need to be a successful seller. A broker who says what you want to hear, may also stretch the truth with a buyer and this can have serious consequences for you, the seller.*

❖ *Verify the prospective broker's abilities by obtaining contact information and then getting in touch with five or more references – people for whom the broker has worked in the past couple of years.*

❖ *It is absolutely critical that you and your broker have excellent communication. You need to have realistic expectations, and your broker needs to keep you informed of what's going on with your offering. Without the ability to work together, you and your broker are less likely to achieve a successful sale of your business.*

❖ *You can define some aspects of your relationship with a broker in the listing agreement. If the contract calls for the broker to be in touch with you a minimum number of times each week and to spend a specified amount to advertise your business for sale, it is clear what you expect. Ultimately, it will be easier to work with the broker, and probably more productive as well, with expectations expressed at the beginning and communication made a contractual part of your relationship.*

❖ *While it may not be critical that your broker is a "specialist" in your type of business, it is important that he or she is not too busy with a "stable" of listings, and thereby unable to give your offering the time and attention needed to find a buyer and achieve a sale.*

❖ *A six-month listing is long enough to get your small California business exposed to the market and make sure your broker is properly representing you. Don't agree to have the listing go longer than that, so you won't be committed to someone who is not working effectively. A listing can always be extended after three or six months if you're satisfied with the work of the broker.*

❖ *Brokers, like everyone else, hate surprises. Make sure to let your representative know about weaknesses or deficiencies in your small California business so the problem can be addressed. The "bad" news may not impair the marketability of your business. But if the broker and a buyer find out that you weren't completely forthcoming about important information, it will impact your ability to sell.*

CHAPTER SEVEN

HOW TO SET THE PRICE THAT'S RIGHT - 1

Most every operation involved in preparing your small California business for sale requires a logical approach and methodical execution. Follow the correct steps in sequence and you'll be ready to wow the market with your offering.

Well, there's one exception to this principle of using a scientific method, and that's the requirement for setting the proper value for the business.

Many economists and investment experts who've studied the problem – trying to apply any one of several valuation methods – have concluded that there's as much art as there is science in establishing a value for a small business. Some even consider the process to be a form of magic.

Pricing correctly is a challenge, and most everyone who studies the issue has a preferred method. But no single approach offers a definitive way to place a value on a business that will accurately predict, every time, what the market says it is worth.

Are you a disciple of the replacement value method? What about looking at a small California business from the point of view of an investor, or a tax accountant? Is book value the way to go? What about liquidated value plus some money allocated to goodwill? Is there such a thing as "going business value"; or is this idea about as useful as the conclusions reached by ancient theologians who argued about how many angels can fit on the head of a pin?

And yes, it's true that the value of a small business is exactly the sum that the willing buyer and seller – free of undue pressure – agree on, but how can the dollar amount applied to that company give us a clue as to the right price for any other business?

We'll explore that question in this chapter and focus on a major yardstick for measuring value – what is called "adjusted net income,' also described as "seller's discretionary cash flow." Then we'll review a couple of standard valuation approaches as well as performance and market–determined ways to arrive at the proper selling price for your small California business.

In the following chapter, HOW TO SET THE PRICE THAT'S RIGHT - 2, we'll discover the ways that other parts of a deal for the sale of a business exert an influence on selling price.

It's Not Real Estate

As we've noted before, it's a mistake to use principles involved in the sale of real property to resolve questions pertaining to sale of a business.

If the public had access to a database of actual prices recently paid for small California businesses, and if there was some uniformity about small businesses and one accounting method used in each case, perhaps we could rely on the comparables approach to valuation. It works well in the real estate market. The selling price of your neighbor's house is an excellent reference point to use as you determine the value of yours.

But none of these conditions exist. There is no place to look up selling prices of businesses. And no two businesses are alike.

To emphasize this point, an executive employed by a fast food franchisor tells a story about one of the company's franchisees who owned two businesses in a Southern California community. In most every respect, the businesses were identical. They had been built at about the same time for nearly identical costs, and they were located just over a mile apart, in very similar areas, each in a retail strip center surrounded by mid-priced residential development. As the owner was involved in day-to-day operations of both, the management was the same.

And yet one of the businesses averaged a few dollars more in profit most every month over a two year period. It took careful analysis to determine that minor variations in traffic patterns tended to yield slightly higher gross revenues in the more profitable of the two. And the less profitable store had been affected by a series of unexpected problems, such as a power outage that affected the area and a broken sewer line that required businesses on that block to be closed for a couple of days.

These small and subtle differences, however, became big factors when the owner decided to sell. He put each on the market separately, and received about $100,000 more for the slightly more profitable business. The executive concludes the example by noting that had the properties been homes, instead of businesses in the area, any small differences between them would have been expressed as a tiny variation in selling price – not the six figure difference that occurred in the case of the sold businesses.

Considering the lack of comparables to aid in valuation of small businesses – the way homes and other real estate properties can be assigned asking prices – how does an owner determine the correct amount to ask for his or her small California business; particularly when the experts can't even agree?

And It's Not a Passive Investment

A seller who makes the mistake of comparing the purchase of her small California company to an investment in the stock market – where multiples are several times the figures we've discussed – has forgotten that the typical purchaser is buying a career and will work in the business.

An investment in a public company might be several times annual earnings per share, but the investor is doing nothing to contribute to that value. At the same time, the buyer of a small California business is actually earning his or her salary by the work of managing the company, calling on prospective clients, running the equipment, answering the phone, dealing with an unhappy customer and sweeping the floors. As far as the buyer is concerned, every penny received is well earned.

When the purchase price of your business is considered from this perspective, a buyer could claim that there is no return on the investment but that the income is entirely a result of the owner's labor. You might disagree, and claim that the new owner can hire someone to handle those responsibilities. Under this scenario, of course, the buyer's income from the business will be dramatically reduced by the size of the salary paid to the key employee, which then reduces the cash flow to a trickle.

A smart buyer will then point out that he can get the same return by buying common stock in a blue-chip company. He's almost certain to get the anticipated earnings with no work and without the headaches and risks that go with small business ownership.

This very argument between seller and buyer has taken place many times when there was a disagreement about value. It demonstrates how the purchase of a business differs from a passive investment and why an intelligent seller of a small California business should have an understanding of the realities in the marketplace in order to correctly price a company for sale.

Put Yourself In the Buyer's Wallet

The best way to gain a clear marketplace perspective is recommended by experienced business brokers, rejecting complex theoretical approaches in favor of the most common principles they can derive from completed deals. Their idea is to focus on two major dynamics: One, the expectations of a small business buyer; and two, how well a subject business performs in relation to the expectations. And then there are a number of factors which help to adjust the basic value to reflect all the realities of the market and the situation.

Actually this way of trying to set a correct price is a variation on the theories of many economists who subscribe to the discounted value of future earnings principle. So there is support for this idea among traditional analysts.

The first part of this approach is to understand a typical buyer's expectations regarding purchase of a small business. Remembering that most buyers of small businesses in California are seeking to – as one broker puts it – "buy a job," it would be useful to analyze the issue from that perspective.

Calculate ROI for Owner/Operator

"How much money do you want to make?" That is usually one of the first questions a business broker will ask of a new buyer client.

And the answer, for most buyers is: "As much as I can and certainly enough to support my family."

Whether that figure is $50,000 per year, or $75,000, or $200,000 or $456,000, the buyer will soon learn that what he or she must pay will be a function of the income desired. And the value of a business tends to form around this central theme. If buyers in a particular area feel that they should get back their investment in say, two years of owning, operating and working in the subject business, then their "right" price will be twice the annual output of cash and cash equivalents that flow to the owner. If they are prepared to wait for three years' work in the business before the investment is recovered, then the business will sell for a multiple of three times annual cash flow.

This principle does, of course, raise a few key questions, that should be addressed as part of this discussion. The questions are: How is the multiple determined? Exactly how does a buyer measure cash flow? And what about the terms of a deal – does the amount of cash required influence the use of a multiple?

Multiple of earnings

This idea is largely a reflection of supply and demand. In the California market for small businesses, during the past several years, people purchasing a means of livelihood, have been willing to go along with an asking a price that exceeds a year's income from that business. But in most cases they have not been willing to pay more than a multiple of three to four times the earnings in the most recent year. And to complete this balance of market forces, most sellers have been in agreement with this formula. The meeting of demand and supply forces at the range of approximately two to three times annual cash flow has established the market rate that has prevailed in California through the past few decades.

A number of factors go into this equation, of course. And if circumstances were to change substantially, the multiple might change as well. For example, a profound improvement in the state's economy might reduce the risk involved in taking over a business, which could have the effect of raising the multiple. If buyers were more certain that they would be successful in their new business, and anticipated a strong likelihood of rapid growth, they might be willing to pay four or more times current annual income as a purchase price.

An example of the reverse effect would be an improvement in the employment conditions in the state. With companies paying high salaries and providing substantial benefits to lure workers, there might be fewer active candidates ready to purchase in the small business market. This would likely result in a reduction of the multiple as businesses lowered asking prices in the competition for buyers.

Measuring Cash Flow: Adjusted Net Income aka Seller's Discretionary Cash Flow

If all small California businesses were required to use a standard set of accounting practices – something like the rules applied by the Securities and Exchange Commission (SEC) for publicly traded corporations – it would be fairly easy to determine cash flow. And this could apply to the local fried chicken franchise, the carpet cleaning service, the soft drink bottling company, the shoe-shine stand on the corner and every other owner operated enterprise. But that's not the case. (And considering that so many small business entrepreneurs are adamant about doing things their own way, it's unlikely that the imposition of a single system of accounting rules for them will ever be adopted.)

Examples of the inconsistencies in reporting methods are plentiful. Many closely held corporations continue to show losses on the books, even though the owners are able to live quite lavishly. And other businesses report profits, yet their owners can't find as much as a dime in the cash drawer.

As a business owner, you recognize that there are cash benefits to your operation which are not reflected on the profit and loss statement. If you add up items such as the company paid car and insurance (to the extent covering non-business travel), the funds set aside for depreciation that exceed actual replacement expenses, and the inventory and equipment that have been written off the books but still exist, you will arrive at a sum that can be considered your "add backs." This figure, added to the profit shown for your business represents the cash flow you would report when selling your business.

Since there are so many ways to conduct this calculation, you'll have a hard time finding a single formula that applies in all cases and exactly matches the circumstances of your business. Your accountant or a skilled business broker will be able to help you determine the figure you can call "adjusted net income", when your business is offered for sale.

At the end of this chapter is a P & L statement from a hypothetical business. This would be submitted with the corporate tax return. And there's a "recast" P&L noting which expense categories listed under the heading of operating costs, actually describe funds that don't get spent on the business, but go to the owner. These funds don't look like profits on the financial statement, and they aren't subject to the taxation that is imposed on profits, but they are used to benefit the owner just the same. See the P & L and "Recast" P & L at the end of this chapter.

We need the total of all these funds if we're to establish a business value based on the most important criteria used in valuation – the amount of money the owner will receive from the business – that is, the adjusted net income.

Cash requirements can influence the value

The terms of a deal almost always impact what a buyer is willing to pay for a business. If you insist on an all-cash transaction, for example, you might expect to receive up to 25% less than the price you would get if you financed one-third to one-half the price. One explanation for this is that fewer buyers will have ready funds to meet your requirements and have working capital. So you'll need to shave the price to meet a smaller buyer pool.

Another explanation is that the multiple used in pricing a business is influenced by risk. Having to put up the entire purchase price of a business, carries with it an increased risk of loss, or at least the perception of an increase in the risk – maybe because the seller's insistence on all cash is an indication he thinks you won't succeed.

Naturally, the size of the cash down payment required is only one factor with an impact on business valuation. We'll discuss other influences on value later in this chapter.

Compare to Start-up Costs for Industry Insiders

As mentioned in a previous chapter, the purchasers who plan to work in their new companies and who expect the profits to provide their livelihood, represent some 80% of the buyers active in the California market for small businesses.

Their approach to valuation is consistent with their financial abilities, their needs and expectations.

The other type of buyer you may encounter, as noted earlier, is a company in your industry. But that buyer will approach the valuation of your offering in a different way.

Once again, you're encouraged to pretend you are the buyer – a manager at a company in your industry – who is looking at your business as a possible acquisition. By assuming this point of view, it will be easier for you to understand the approach to valuation that applies in this situation.

Such a buyer is less interested in using a multiples of cash flow approach because it doesn't really address the realities of the purchase. For one thing, the cash flow you have experienced will change dramatically for the new owner, because of the consolidation that will result from the acquisition. Most likely your assets will be pooled with those of the acquiring company, so that everything is under one roof – yours or theirs. And they may not need all of your employees, as they have people already in the business functions that can take over the work of some of the people who were on your payroll. These moves may substantially reduce the costs to which you are accustomed, and boost the bottom line.

These differences are among the reasons that an industry insider considering the idea of acquiring your firm will not value your business the same way as will the buyer who intends to take over as the owner/operator.

Instead, the insider's calculations tend to focus on what it would cost to replace your assets and to service your customers. Considering that the goal is to roughly duplicate your company, if it would be cheaper to buy your business than start from scratch, then you can expect an offer. But that's unlikely. In most cases, the company already in the business is not interested in the entire going operation you have for sale, but in segments of it. That might include a customer list and some equipment. And they may be glad to hire one or more of your most able employees but probably won't be willing to pay you for the privilege.

The industry insider will be unwilling to pay the premium for "entry to the industry." That's what you're more likely to get from an independent buyer.

These differences are useful for a seller to know, so that you can understand the variations in valuation approach and how that will affect what buyers are willing to pay for your business.

Price Adjustments: Terms of the Deal, Extra Assets, Unusual Circumstances, Quick Sale

These ideas about valuing a company are useful in establishing a basc line – the initial figure – that can then be adjusted, plus or minus, according to other factors introduced into the equation.

The characteristics that can alter the starting point of value determination might be as varied and numerous as there are kinds of businesses. For our purposes however, there are a few common issues impacting the value of a business that deserve our attention.

It was noted earlier that the terms of a deal can influence the final number. And we'll take up that matter in some detail in the next chapter.

And rather than cite only examples of over-priced listings, I might mention that there have been plenty of instances where buyers bought a company at below-market values having been in the right place at the right time. This can occur when a sale must be completed quickly because of death or illness of a principal. And the increased motivation of the seller for any number of reasons, can result in a lower price than might have been accepted under normal circumstances.

If a capital infusion will be needed soon after the buyer takes over – to replace faltering equipment, for example – the business selling price might be depressed as a result. And the reverse is true. Sometimes an abundance of capital equipment can help a seller ask for and get a higher price than the usual multiple might dictate. The seller would argue that there's more assets to sell if needed, thereby reducing the business's downside risk. Besides, the additional machinery might enable the company to be even more productive and efficient and further prolong the useful life of the company's present infrastructure. A seller might also be able to boost the selling price a bit by promising to stay on without pay for awhile to help manage and to insure the buyer's success.

Is your business in a growth industry? Does your business confer on the owner any special opportunities or benefits that make it particularly desirable? These and other positive factors can result in a multiple of four or higher, being used to assess the value of what you have to sell.

Making your business less interesting, of course, is a short term lease for a location-sensitive enterprise, a declining market for your products or services, and other conditions that might increase the risk and/or reduce the appeal of your company.

Another set of factors have to do with the ease of management. If most anyone can stand behind the cash register and collect money, there will be a larger market of potential buyers and hence, a willingness to pay a higher price for your convenience store or retail shop. If special skills or particularly long hours are involved in running the business, however, its value probably will be negatively impacted.

And what about businesses that can be run absentee? If the seller truly does not need to be present for much of the day, the business might command a higher price than one that demands full time involvement on the part of the owner.

These are a few examples of factors that can influence the price of a business – probably just the tip of an iceberg-sized history of how buyer and seller accommodations and changes have affected values in transactions for small businesses in California.

It might be instructive also for sellers to be aware of a couple of pricing strategies that are helpful if you want to get the full value for your company and aren't satisfied with the approaches suggested.

The Earn Out

Perhaps the best way to explain this way of defining the price of a business is by giving an example of the Northern California distribution company that was sold according to an earn-out formula.

Because this well established firm was highly profitable, and required very little in the way of working capital, the owner asked a price that was nearly five times the annual income he collected.

The buyer was very impressed with the operation but a bit worried about the fact that there were virtually no hard assets to be included. If he were to fail, there would be nothing of value remaining from his investment.

The final deal called for half the price to be paid in cash, with the seller taking back the balance over a five year period. It was agreed that the remaining amount owed on the business would be adjusted according to the buyer's subsequent profit. If the business was as lucrative over the payoff period as the seller promised, the seller would receive his full purchase price with interest. If there was a drop-off in earnings, the seller's payments would be adjusted downward, accordingly. It was a workable solution for parties to the agreement because it addressed their issues. The broker, however, was frustrated with this approach, as his commission was based on the purchase price and he had to wait 60 months to finish collecting his fee.

Letting the Market Determine Price

This strategy, perhaps inspired by techniques for selling real estate during hot markets, involves setting a deadline for offers, then inviting all interested buyers to submit the top price they're willing to pay by that date. This is similar to an auction with all interested participants encouraged to submit their maximum bid. The method works best in a situation where there are a number of prospective buyers who are motivated to own the company being offered. The benefit for the seller is that the maximum price might come out of this competitive process, without the need for a lot of negotiations and the risk of selling too low, too quickly. While this can be an effective tactic to achieve the desired ends, it should be handled by a broker experienced in this type of sale, so as to keep it orderly and to complete it successfully.

Valuing Unreported Income

Some sellers, while discussing the value of their business, get on the subject of having a buyer pay for income not recognized anywhere in the business' books. They want to know how that can be done.

My advice: Forget about it!

There are a number of reasons that you don't want to discuss unreported income with a purchaser, beginning with the fact that your prospective buyer may be an IRS agent engaged in the government's campaign to catch tax cheats. If you're still not convinced it's a bad idea to brag to a buyer about the money you siphon, consider the possibility of a disagreement with that person resulting in a lawsuit.

Will you settle up at less-than-favorable terms so the other party doesn't spill your secret? Or will you go to court and watch the judge, jury, attorneys and witnesses hear testimony about how you explained the technique you've developed for laundering cash in your business?

And even if there are no consequences on the order of a legal dispute, do you really want to have a good buyer learn about your dishonesty and then worry about your trustworthiness in the rest of the deal?

You can't have it both ways. If you're realizing net income without tax consequences it's not appropriate to claim it as part of your cash flow. If you want to sell your small California business based on the total of your earnings, they should show up in your records.

Conclusion

A discussion of this subject – setting the right price at which to sell your business – could easily fill volumes of textbooks. For our purposes, the objective is to provide a brief overview.

A useful way for the seller to understand how to properly value a business is to look at the problem from the point of view of an independent buyer who will work in the business as the owner/operator. Using this perspective, you can see what the buyer anticipates will be the return on investment of time and labor. And you'll likely understand more clearly what a buyer needs and expects when contemplating the purchase of your offering.

The individual buyer's approach is different from that of the way your company will be valued by someone in the industry who might want to acquire your business and consolidate it with another firm. Because this purchase may only involve part of what you offer – customers and some hard assets, for example – you can expect a quicker deal, but a lower selling price, reflecting the reduced value your business has to this kind of buyer.

A few examples of factors influencing a company's value and a couple of strategies for determining value in a dynamic marketplace are offered to provide the seller with some guidelines for establishing the right price at which to sell his or her small California business.

And sellers who wonder how to include unreported cash for purposes of pricing their business are advised to forget it!

KEY POINTS FROM THIS CHAPTER

❖ Pricing a business correctly for sale continues to be a challenge with many economists and finance experts offering different theories about how to do it.

❖ It's a mistake to use principles involving the valuation of real property to try to determine what a small California business is worth. That's because there is no way to research selling prices of businesses, and anyway, no two businesses are comparable.

❖ The best approach toward valuation for sale to an independent buyer is to pretend you are that person and imagine what your expectations might be.

❖ Calculating a multiple of the earnings is a useful way to compute a business's value as it represents a balance of market supply and demand.

❖ Also a subject of differing opinions is the matter of measuring cash flow. A seller might benefit by discussing with an accountant or experienced business broker how to determine this figure for his or her business.

❖ Influencing values are a number of factors including risk, the terms of a deal (how much cash down is required), future of the industry, involvement of the seller, ease of management, amount of working capital that will be needed, and other issues that can impact success for the new owner.

❖ Review the next chapter for more ideas and information about how the terms of a transaction often can influence its price.

❖ If considering a sale to another company in your industry, recognize that the valuation approach will be different than that of an independent buyer. Industry insiders will want only some of your assets and probably will pay a lower price.

❖ The Earn Out strategy may help a buyer and seller arrive at a program for sale of the company that protects the buyer on the downside, and rewards the seller for the continuation of robust revenues.

❖ Some sellers can avoid negotiations and, perhaps, achieve the maximum price obtainable, when they ask that interested buyers make their best offer by a certain date. This is a bid process that should be handled only by experienced brokers.

❖ There's a simple answer for sellers wondering how to "price" the business' income that doesn't get reported: It is, "forget it!"

Phiquex Manufacturing

Profit and Loss FY 2004

Category	Item	$ Amount	%
INCOME			
	From operations	626,812.00	
	Other (consulting)	11,000.00	
	Returns/Allowances	486.00	
	Gross Revenues	**$637,326.00**	**1.00**
EXPENSES			
	Cost of Goods:		
	Labor	190,405.60	0.299
	Materials	81,577.72	0.128
	Total	271,983.32	.427
	Gross Profit	**$365,342.68**	
	Overhead:		
	Advertising/promotion	8,922.56	0.014
	Administrative	7,647.91	0.012
	Auto	5,735.93	0.009
	Bank Charges	637.32	0.001
	Depreciation/Ammort	10,834.54	0.017
	Health coverage	13,383.84	0.021
	Insurance	19,757.10	0.031
	Interest	10,197.21	0.016
	Janitorial	25,493.04	0.04
	Legal/Accounting	12,109.19	0.019
	Maintenance	7,010.58	0.011
	Miscellaneous	7,647.91	0.012
	Office/Computer	14,021.17	0.022
	Officer Salary	18,000.00	0.028
	Payroll services	4,461.28	0.007
	Rent	52,898.06	0.083
	Selling Expenses	12,746.52	0.02
	Shipping/Handling	17,207.80	0.027
	Supplies	11,471.88	0.018
	Travel	3,823.96	0.006
	Utilities	29,954.32	0.047
	Total Expenses	**$293,962.12**	**0.461**
Net Income		**$ 71,380.56**	**0.112**

Phiquex Manufacturing

Table of Add Backs to Compute Adjusted Net Income (Recast Financials)

Advertising/promotion	8,922.56	Sponsored Little League Team	1,200.00
Administrative	7,647.91	Sister's help running errands	3,250.00
Auto	5,735.93	Personal use est. 80%	4,589.00
Bank Charges	637.32		
Depreciation/Ammort	10,834.54	50% unneeded reserve	5,417.27
Health coverage	13,383.84	For officer and family	13,383.84
Insurance	19,757.10		
Interest	10,197.21		
Janitorial	25,493.04		
Legal/Accounting	12,109.19	Est. 25% for officer's personal	3,027.30
Maintenance	7,010.58		
Miscellaneous	7,647.91		
Office/Computer	14,021.17		
Officer Salary	18,000.00	Officer Salary	18,000.00
Payroll services	4,461.28		
Rent	52,898.06		
Selling Expenses	12,746.52	Personal Entertainment ($300/mo)	3,600.00
Shipping/Handling	17,207.80		
Supplies	11,471.88		
Travel	3,823.96	50% personal travel at trade show	1,912.00
Utilities	29,954.32		
Net Income	**$71,380.56**	**Total Add Backs**	**$54,379.41**
		Adjusted Net Income (Net Income + Total Add Backs)	**$125,759.97**

PLEASE NOTE THAT THIS INFORMATION REPRESENTS THE IDEAS OF THE SELLER AS TO WHAT CONSTITUTES ADJUSTED NET INCOME. BUYERS ARE URGED TO DISCUSS THIS ANALYSIS WITH THEIR ACCOUNTANTS AND TO DISCUSS WITH TAX ATTORNEYS THE TAX IMPLICATIONS REGARDING THE REPORTING OF INFORMATION.

THE SELLER DOES NOT REPRESENT THAT HE IS GIVING OUT, IN THE CONTEXT OF THIS INFORMATION, ANY ACCOUNTING OR TAX ADVICE.

CHAPTER EIGHT

HOW TO SET THE PRICE THAT'S RIGHT - 2

Having reviewed some approaches to pricing a small California business in the previous chapter, and having touched on key pricing components, such as Adjusted Net Income, it's now appropriate to focus on pricing in a more macroeconomic sense. Specifically, it's important for sellers to understand pricing in terms of what you really are striving for in a sale – maximum economic benefit.

There can, in fact, be a difference between getting your price when the deal is signed, and still being satisfied – perhaps months or years later – that you received the best possible return from the sale of your business.

Price is a Piece of the Puzzle

A knowledgeable escrow holder with whom I sometimes work, likes to portray pricing as a piece of the puzzle – an important piece to be sure – but not the entire picture. In the course of a business offering, the final price might be the seller's prime consideration. Many sellers relish the moment when they announce at the country club or to a proud family that they got $1 million (or some other magic number) for the business. But talk to the seller some time later, after the IRS is through, and the attorney calls about the fallout created by the imminent failure of the business because the buyer is overextended, and you may hear an entirely different story.

It is because of the importance of other issues involved and intertwined with the question of establishing price, that the entire picture needs to be brought to the attention of sellers as you market your small California businesses.

Establishing the Down payment

If a buyer has the opportunity to leverage into a business with a down payment and a promise to pay the balance to the seller over a period of time, there's more incentive to make the purchase. That will translate into a higher price than an all cash requirement.

The down payment can influence price the way a cash requirement affects the desirability of anything that's for sale. As you crank up the down payment threshold, the number of qualified and interested buyers dwindles. And that translates immediately into softer demand which, in turn, tends to bring down the value of what's offered. The lesson of this economic principle for a business seller is that if you want to get your substantial price, you need to be flexible on the terms by which that price is paid.

Do you believe in the future of your business? If you insist on most of the cash at the close of escrow, it may be for any number of reasons. But regardless of your rationale, the buyer is likely to conclude that you want out, with minimum ties, because you see doom ahead. That's not a healthy message to send when someone's considering the purchase of your business.

In consultations with sellers who seemed determined that they needed all or most of the purchase price in the down payment, I've learned that in most cases their underlying agenda could be addressed with an alternative to the lots-of-cash solution.

The seller of a bookstore in central California, for example, wanted a sizable down payment, and after some discussion, explained that she needed to retire the debt on the company's computer system and inventory management software, and to eliminate a payables balance to vendors. "I want to make sure everything is free and clear for a new buyer," she explained.

The answer to this problem was, of course, quite simple. The obligations represented a neat little financing vehicle. Included in the price was the assumption of the seller's debt. With a more reasonable offering package, she was able to find a buyer who was pleased with the low down payment requirement. He used his cash to invest in a promotion campaign which improved the store's sales. And he was able to quickly pay off the debt that he'd assumed.

Other sellers have maintained they needed the purchase price all at once because the money way earmarked for an investment – in one case the down payment on a retirement home; another seller had his eye on an expensive European sports car. Once the reasons for the cash down payment requirements were voiced, we were able to develop a strategy that met their needs, including getting their businesses sold. Each seller raised the needed money from a bank and serviced the new debt using payments coming from the buyer under their freshly-minted seller financing programs.

Sellers may complain that this adds a bit of work and may cost a few dollars in the interest spread (between what is paid to the lender and collected from the buyer) but most see these costs as well worth the benefit of a completed deal at the desired price.

And I've heard sellers object, bluntly, to financing a deal because of the fear the buyer won't succeed in the business and will fail to make payments. That's not a happy prospect. It makes me wonder if it's time to restructure the offering to reflect the seller's bleak outlook. Or maybe a more competent buyer will solve the problem.

Incidentally, sellers whose businesses require a lot of working capital will be more likely to get their price by offering the buyer easy terms. For example, if the new owner will have to finance receivables and carry a large inventory, the seller will be more likely to get his asking price if it can be handled with a down payment that is one-half or less, and manageable terms for the balance. A seller who forgets about the cash needs of an incoming owner, and who forgets that the new owner will want to measure the return against the entire cash outlay (not just the down payment) is likely to set a price that's out of reach of the market.

I'm a strong advocate for seller financing being part of a transaction whenever possible – particularly considering that the majority of sellers who think they need most of their cash at the start, actually have alternatives. The biggest need for cash when an enterprise changes hands is usually with the business itself, so the buyer can deal with unexpected expenses and invest in promoting to generate more business. When sellers think through this issue, they generally agree that the continuation of the business in a healthy state is in their best interests.

How Payments to a Seller Can be Structured

Not only down payment, but other aspects of a deal structure can impact the price. In the midst of a marketing campaign involving a Sacramento area dry cleaning business a few years ago, a layer of uncertainty was added to the mix when the seller's landlord announced plans for a major remodel of the shopping center. Had this action been imminent, the seller might have elected to wait out the construction and disruption of business, and then re-energize his selling efforts once the facility was back in full operation. But the project wasn't scheduled to begin for 18 months, and might be delayed beyond that. The seller, suffering health problems and eager to retire, was uncertain what to tell prospective buyers. They wanted to know, of course, not only when the construction would begin, but also how long it would go on and what impact it would have on business. And although the landlord had promised to offer tenants some rent relief to lessen the impact of lost revenue, it was not clear how helpful that would be.

When an interested and motivated buyer was found, a deal was worked out with seller financing for half the purchase price over a four year period. It was agreed that during the construction, the buyer's monthly payments to the seller would be reduced by a ratio equal to the percentage drop-off in business recorded the prior month. For example, if the August sales were 25% less than the prior August, the buyer's September payment would be 75% of the standard monthly amount. In this case, the final selling price would not be determined until the end of the four-year obligation. But by allowing payments – and ultimately, the price – to "float" with business revenues, the seller was able to conclude a transaction in a timely manner, even in the face of these future unknowns.

In some circumstances where a new owner would be strapped for cash for the first few months after taking over, there has been cooperation by sellers agreeing to wait three months, even six months before the buyer was required to begin making payments on the obligation created by seller financing. Another approach has been designed for a situation where a business risks failure at some future time. Perhaps a big-box competitor is rumored to be moving into the area. Maybe the landlord has not yet committed to a lease renewal past the expiration coming in a few years. The reasoning in these cases is that if the worst happens, the seller would have been out of business anyway. So provisions can be included in the sales contract allowing the buyer to call for cancellation of the seller-financed note, and stop making payments, if the business must be discontinued or cut back dramatically.

This creative approach usually includes a low price because of the risk that the buyer won't have a business to sell, and eventually will lose the investment. But, of course, the price isn't definitive until the end of the obligation to the seller, because price is related to the payments which can be altered based on what happens in the future.

There also are small business transactions in California in which the price is modified in the upward direction, after close of escrow, in response to a change in circumstances that confer a substantial benefit to the business. A Southern California construction business was sold that way. The sellers turned over the business to a new owner before they learned whether their bid on a lucrative government project, with a long lead time, would be accepted. Their sales contract with the buyer called for a balloon payment to be made to sellers 90 days after awarding of the contract, if it went to their company.

In these situations the right price is a changeable number, meant to reflect real circumstances over time. Although it isn't the solution in every case in which there are questions about what will happen in the future – and not everyone is flexible enough to see the benefits of this approach – it is a very effective way to please the buyer and seller who want their agreed-on price to be correct today as well as tomorrow.

The interaction of price and seller terms in a transaction for a small California business can impact the way a note is structured.

Suppose a seller reluctantly agrees to carry back part of a purchase price on a profitable business so the buyer can use her limited cash to fuel the company's continued growth. The payoff might be set up with large payments over a short period of time – that is, the debt is retired quickly. The benefit for the buyer is avoiding a cash-strapping down payment so there's money to make sure the business stays on a success track. And the seller wins with a satisfactory transaction, the payoff handled rather rapidly, plus the likelihood that the business – which secures the debt – will remain strong.

In many of these cases, as the terms are adjusted, the price is affected as well. It's not unusual for a fast payoff schedule – as in the example just cited – to be linked with a lowered price. And the reverse can be true. If the seller agrees to let the buyer take plenty of time retiring the financing, the incentive might be expressed in a full-price deal. In effect, the seller is saying: "Okay, you can stretch out my payments and make your monthly obligation pretty low, but you have to meet my price."

What is the Best Collateral for the Seller Who Carries Back

Another piece of the puzzle forming the picture of a complete transaction has to do with the choice of collateral. In other words, what will secure the debt to a seller who finances part of the purchase price? In most cases a note to the seller is collateralized by the assets of the business. And that's usually fine with the buyer. "After all," the purchaser reasons, "if the seller believes the business is good, he should have no problem about accepting it as security for the loan."

Not every seller sees it this way, however. Consider someone who's built a successful, profitable small California business and now wants to retire, expecting the proceeds from the business sale to provide the funds needed for the seller's later years. The outgoing owner has agreed to carry back part of the purchase price to make the business more desirable and to yield a good selling price. The problem comes in when it's the business itself that is suggested as security for what will be the major portion of the seller's income.

The seller in this case has a concern – a legitimate one – that the retirement planning, everything worked for over years of building the business, is riding on the success of the new owner. Suppose the owner fails, through no fault of the business. There can be a health problem, a natural disaster and any number of circumstances that would have the effect of ruining the seller's financial future. "How about a piece of property? Maybe your home?" suggests the seller.

As you might observe, both parties have a legitimate concern. What to do? The place for compromise might be in the sales price. And indeed, the solution sometimes is an adjustment in price to reflect the risk/reward dynamic involved in this dilemma. If granted the concession of a lower price for the business, the buyer might be willing to put up a piece of real estate, such as a second mortgage on the family home, to satisfy the seller's feelings of insecurity. Alternatively, a boosted price might make the seller breath easier about this issue, and be willing to assume the risk, because of the enhanced reward.

Another way to deal with this problem is to have part, but not all of the obligation to the seller backed up with collateral other than the business. The buyer can agree to make payments on two notes, one of which is collateralized by the subject business, the other backed up by a trust deed in real property or the pledge of other assets.

Tax Impact of a Business Sale Affects Pricing

Stephen, owner of a manufacturing company in a suburb of Oakland, had a round figure in mind that he wanted to net from the sale of his business. Most of the people willing to meet his price felt that much of the value of the enterprise resided in his contacts in the industry. Their offers allocated much of the price to his agreement to introduce the new owner to customers, and his promise to refrain from engaging in that business as a competitor for five years following close. The problem, as Stephen learned from his tax accountant, is that the IRS would consider the money allocated this way to be a salary, and it would be subject to taxation as ordinary income – at a high rate.

He'd hoped to have a buyer agree to the idea that purchase of his equipment would represent most of the price. He could then deduct the equipment's book value from the allocated amount, and the difference would be subject to taxation at the lower, capital gains rate. That way he'd net what he wanted.

Because Stephen's method of allocation was not beneficial to the interested buyers, they declined to meet his requirement.

He finally worked out a deal designed to allow Stephen to get the most after-tax benefit from the sale. The allocation was skewed toward Stephen's preferred tax structure, but meant he had to lower his price. He didn't meet his goal but came as close as possible given the tax situation. And the key was the downward adjustment in the total value of the assets – in other words a lower price.

Flexibility Helps Achieve Agreements

A nice round number to brag about. Security for the golden years. The knowledge that the business will continue to be healthy. A good income for the next few years. Keeping the largest share of the sale proceeds allowable under tax law.

These and other considerations enter into the planning you must do when placing your company on the market for sale, and when determining the value – that is, the price to ask for the business.

As the reader has likely determined, the sales price for a business is not set in a vacuum. It is a function of this overall package of benefits for the buyer and seller. The transaction, as a whole, has to meet the needs of the parties in order for them to be in agreement. Otherwise, no deal.

The most successful sellers keep in mind their ultimate objective: Selling the business and receiving the maximum economic benefit warranted by all of the circumstances involved at the time.

There's no value in almost selling the business at a terrific price. Nor does a seller want to get a deal that doesn't yield at least most of the economic benefit anticipated.

Conclusion

Over the past two chapters we've reviewed the issue of price as it applies to the sale of a small California business. First we analyzed the methods of assigning value and the components that are used in the computations when pricing a company. In this chapter the reader is offered several examples to illustrate the way price is merely one component in an overall business transaction. It's one piece of the puzzle. As the real goal of most sellers is to enjoy the maximum possible economic benefit when someone buys your business, you are encouraged to understand the interaction of the payment terms, the tax treatment, and the deal structure that can work with price to help you achieve your objective.

KEY POINTS FROM THIS CHAPTER

❖ *It is important that sellers understand the pricing of a small California business in terms of what you really are striving for in a sale – maximum economic benefit.*

❖ *Down payment relates to price of a business the way that the amount of cash required to buy anything affects the marketability of what's being sold. The more cash needed, the fewer likely buyers. And that can mean a lower value.*

❖ *My experience is that most sellers who think they need all or most of the price of a business as down payment, can find other ways to meet their cash needs. It usually is to their benefit to take less down and provide financing.*

❖ *I advocate seller financing wherever possible as I've learned it usually leads to successful deals where the business continues in a healthy condition and all parties win.*

❖ *Not only down payment, but other aspects of a deal structure can impact price. A transaction for a dry cleaning company example was offered to illustrate how the price was dependent on future events, and was changed through the mechanism of adjustable payments that were influenced by these events.*

❖ *Another example involves the story of a construction company sale that used a balloon payment to adjust the price upward in the event the seeds planted by the sellers were harvested by the buyer.*

❖ *Other alternatives in deal structure include a fast payoff, which can be balanced with a lower price, or a longer payoff, which can be matched with a higher price.*

❖ *The choice of collateral provided to a seller who carries back some purchase price is another part of a transaction that works together with price. A buyer usually feels the business should represent the security; the seller may want other assets. The resolution of this dilemma can sometimes be found in an adjustment of the price or in a mix of securities.*

❖ *Additionally, tax considerations can result in adjustment of price. One party gaining favorable tax treatment may need to give on the price issue and visa versa. Sellers are advised to remember the final selling price does not define their ultimate benefit. Maximum return on the sale, after taxes, is usually what you're after.*

❖ *The most successful sellers keep their desired objectives in mind and remember there's no value in almost selling the business at a terrific price or in getting a deal that doesn't confer at least close to the maximum economic benefit.*

Promoting Your Business for Sale

The day comes when an athlete concludes the pre-game training and enters the field of competition, when the performer finishes practice and steps onto the stage, when the student closes the books and begins taking an exam. And for the owner of a small California business there is a time to complete the preparations discussed in the preceding pages, and start looking for a buyer.

This is that point.

If you've followed some of the advice and ideas offered – organized your papers, discussed and planned the offering with your attorney and accountant, perhaps selected a broker (if you want professional representation), talked things over with your landlord and other people whose cooperation you'll need, then decided on an asking price, and set out the terms – you have managed most of the things over which you have substantial control. But embarking on the marketing campaign will expose you to the uncertainty in this process. From now on you probably will have less influence than you'd like, not only over the reaction of the market to your business for sale, but also the willingness of prospects to make an offer and of buyers to accept your terms.

So you'll do well to manage, as much as you can, the events and outcome of the marketing efforts. Here are some ideas to guide you in the conduct of your campaign. And you'll likely find this information useful to know even if you are turning the responsibility over to a business broker.

Controlled Exposure

The key to getting the best offer on most anything being sold is, of course, to expose it to the largest possible audience of buyers. In any given population of prospects, a certain percentage will have an interest in your offering. The more prospects who are informed about it, the more possible customers with whom you can work.

One distinguishing characteristic about promoting a small California business for sale however, is the need to practice a high degree of discrimination in the choice of your prospects. Most likely you don't want it generally known that the company is being marketed. It's nearly always a bad business practice to let customers, employees, vendors and competitors discover that the business is for sale, and for them to learn about details of your operation.

The challenge then is to broadcast the availability of your business as widely as possible, still keeping it a secret from those individuals who somehow have a connection with the business. You don't want everyone to know your business is for sale – only those people who have no dealings with your enterprise, and who have the financial capability and other qualifications needed to own it.

This is indeed an interesting marketing problem. And there is no sure fire solution.

But there is a strategy commonly practiced by most sellers and business brokers that has proved, over time, to represent the most effective approach. The idea is to consider your promotion program to be a process conducted in phases. The first phase is launched with a broad, general announcement of the company being for sale, and only the most basic information provided. The final phase is a face-to-face-conference in which a qualified prospective buyer – whom you have ascertained is not an employee, regular customer or known competitor – receives proprietary information about your offering in return for a written promise to treat this information confidentiality, not disclosing it to anyone other than the prospective buyer's advisors. And there are interim phases in which you qualify the prospect, while the prospect is learning more about what you offer and deciding whether to pursue it.

I call this process the "dance." It's based on an exchange of information, the give and take of two parties discovering, little-by-little, if there is a mutual interest in doing business. It can end when one of the two parties, or perhaps both, determines there isn't sufficient interest in pursuing the exchange. At that point the interaction can terminate. The other possible outcome of the dance is that your prospect wants to purchase the business, has the ability to do so, and meets your price and terms, or works out with you a mutually agreeable deal.

The Critical First 30-60 Days

As was mentioned earlier in the text, and can't be repeated often enough, the way your small California business is presented during the first month or two is vital to the success of your sales campaign. Like every other business broker and consultant who's been working in the industry for any length of time, I've seen numerous situations in which a perfectly salable business has not been matched up with a suitable buyer after months of marketing. Usually it's because the seller or the seller's representative "dropped the ball" early in the effort. Seeing the same ad in the paper, week after week, is a clue that the business has been improperly marketed from the beginning. Another clue is to hear from a qualified, serious buyer that a broker or seller neglected to respond to an inquiry about a business being offered. Still another is to learn about buyers becoming impatient as they wait to make an offer on a business as soon as they receive the added information promised, but not delivered, by the seller or seller's representative.

Don't lose good buyers by your lack of preparation or inattentiveness to their requests. The longer your business sits on the market, even if the reason is because of your inattention, the more dubious the offering will appear.

Have you ever declined to purchase something you liked because it seemed "shop worn?" Did you ask: "If this is such a good deal, why hasn't someone else bought it already?" If you've had that experience, you understand how a prospective buyer might be uninterested in purchasing your business simply because it has been available for what seems a long time.

Put off the beginning of your marketing program if you have to wait for more records or a confirmation about a lease request. But don't launch your business sales effort as you would a rocket, then let it sputter out before it has a chance to reach orbit while you try to figure out how to respond to inquiries.

Let's review the basic process of exposing your business, and touch on some of the components that make up your campaign.

Advertising

While some brokers feel that general circulation newspapers represent one of the best vehicles for advertising your business for sale, other say they have unsatisfactory results this way, preferring to rely on online business promotion services, such as **www.bizben.com** Others who specialize in particular kinds of businesses try to focus their marketing campaigns with ads in trade periodicals and with contacts at trade associations. The best strategy, if you have the time, patience, and resources, is to reach as many outlets as possible where you feel you might be able to interest prospective buyers – qualified ones – in your business.

I advocate that sellers commit to a budget of $2,000 to $3,000 for advertising in print and web-based media. It may seem like a big investment, but if you want to get your price and terms, assuming they are reasonably set for what you have to offer, you may need exposure to hundreds or thousands of possible prospects. I don't think it makes sense to try to save a little money when you want to get as many people as possible to investigate your offering. Try to generate a large response, so that when the population is narrowed down, through the introduction and qualification process, there are some who remain interested and able to be your buyer.

Incidentally, one of the requirements you might have for your broker, if you are represented by one, is that he or she spends a certain sum on advertising over the life of the listing. In fact, there's no reason not to get this in writing as part of the listing contract. It's not unusual for a brokerage to earmark a few thousand dollars to promote a listing which is well prepared for a sale and will generate thousands of dollars in commissions if a deal is completed.

The local daily newspapers in California carry thousands of business opportunities, most of which don't get the phone to ring. If you're using the metropolitan papers, make sure to advertise in the Sunday editions, which do the job much more effectively than the daily ads. Yes, the newspaper ad rep will try and convince you that once you've reserved space in the Sunday classifieds, it is very inexpensive to extend your campaign to every day. Problem is, most every serious buyer checks only with the Sunday ads. I suggest saving your money for other opportunities rather than have your ad appear, unseen, at other times of the week.

And whether your ad is distributed in printed or electronic classified sections, or both, make sure it includes the best features of your offering so as to increase the chances of getting good responses. Here are some of the phrases likely to provoke an interest on the part of a buyer and get your phone to ring:

- Absentee owner
- Continued history of earnings growth
- Long established
- Good business records
- Great lease
- Flexible landlord
- Very profitable
- Priced to sell
- Good seller financing
- Low down payment
- Seller training included
- Franchise opportunity
- EZ Terms
- Fortune 500 customers
- Super location
- Excellent, new equipment
- Real estate included

This list of catch phrases is as potent on the Internet as in print. Your ads with a web-based service will probably include more information than the 3 or 4-line newspaper ad. And your Internet advertising can usually include a photo, or the corporate logo, if you're selling a known franchise. The added graphic is helpful in getting attention of prospective buyers, a difficult thing to do considering that in many media there are so many displays competing for a reader's attention.

Broker Network

I recently spoke with a seller who felt that it would not be right to let business brokers know about his business for sale, because he had not listed it with a broker. I don't agree. There's no reason you can't contact brokerages with buyers seeking businesses to let them know what you offer. Some brokers, as mentioned earlier, represent buyers only, and are paid by the buyer upon successful completion of a transaction. The more businesses these brokers are aware of, the better. And there's no reason you can't negotiate with a broker to bring you the eventual buyer for a few percentage points more than you're asking and keep the difference as a fee. You may even be agreeable to the idea of deducting half of a full commission from your proceeds to pay a broker who brings the buyer willing and able to meet your terms.

As you can see, there are a number of ways to approach the idea of getting a broker's help in finding a buyer, even if you are representing yourself and saving the listing brokerage fee. An active business broker has something you don't have – a current database of qualified buyers. By working with a broker, or brokers who would represent the buyer, you can access that resource without having to give up a full brokerage fee.

Meanwhile, don't neglect to connect with chambers of commerce, business networking organizations and other business-related social opportunities to meet prospective buyers or, perhaps someone with a brother-in-law or friend who would be the perfect new owner for your business. I've known sellers to flush out good buyers by doing their networking at alumni groups and even by posting a notice at union halls and vocational schools that teach a curriculum related to the subject of your business. And if your business is a franchise, don't forget to check with your franchisor for leads of people who have inquired about an opportunity in your area.

Initial Qualifying

An early step is for you to establish a way for people to contact you. A dedicated telephone number obtained simply for this purpose will allow you to get calls from interested parties, and they won't know (until you're ready to tell them) whom they're contacting. This is clearly preferable to giving your business phone number (there goes your secret!) or your home number (where your caller will hear the barking dog and blasting video games and then leave a return number with one of the forgetful teens in your house). An answering machine or voice mail message should be attached to the number so if you can't answer, the caller gets a professional reception and is reassured that you'll respond promptly to the request. And then make sure you do so.

If you have a cell phone usually with you, it doesn't hurt to place that number in the ad as well. You can't make it too easy for interested buyers to get in touch with you. You can always reject someone later if they are not serious or are otherwise unqualified. But initially you want to hear from as many people as possible.

Some sellers think it's sufficient to do business out of a post office box, rather than a phone number, as it gives prospects a way to communicate with you without knowing who you are. They appreciate this as quicker to get than a new phone number and less costly. I think this is a mistake. You need to communicate in a way that's easy for people to contact and respond to you. Another possibility is to set up an email account just for this purpose. Some people prefer to communicate this way, so you should have the capability of being reached and of responding to them on the Internet. My preference, however, is the telephone. I believe your communication, if it will lead to a sale, must be immediate and direct.

In your records it's a good idea to keep track of which ads are producing the most and the best calls. You may want to alter the campaign at some point, and the information about what outlets are producing the most and the best responses will help you to de-emphasize unproductive media so you can beef-up the online media or the printed periodicals that are working best for you.

When first talking to the person, whether you answered their call or phoned back after getting a message, you want to learn as much as you can – not only how to get back to them, but also find out what they're looking for.

If you're not in the habit of setting up a file for a project such as selling your business, make a note to yourself that you've just learned a useful idea. One of the folders in the file should contain a list of all the people you talk to, all of the information you've obtained about them and a note about what was discussed and when.

Before spending much time with this person, you want to try and determine if he or she is qualified as to financial ability and the skills to run your business. You also want to determine, right away, if the two of you are able to communicate productively in a way that might lead to a transaction for your business.

If the prospect is completely unwilling to tell you anything about them or their interests, this actually is effective communication. They are letting you know they won't participate in the "dance of information exchange." But it's not communication likely to help you sell the business, so you're probably well advised to cut that conversation short and go on to the next prospect.

We'll cover, in more detail, the questions to ask – and even offer some suggested scripts – when we take up the subject of qualifying prospects in the next chapter.

A response to your ad or an inquiry from a broker or business advisor in touch with possible buyers can all be handled the same way. Many sellers find it useful to send out, or fax (but not from your office), or email a one-page "blind profile" that gives the basic details about your business, without revealing the name, address or enough specifics to identify it (see the blind profile sample at the end of this chapter). Respond to the inquiry with that information, after getting the name and contact details for the person who asked. And encourage the party to contact you if they want to learn more.

Incidentally, I know of sellers who included, with the blind profile, a couple of blank forms – the non-disclosure agreement and a financial statement sheet. They explained that before getting into too much more detail about the business, they would require the non-disclosure commitment and would want to know more about the buyer's ability. I think this is an excellent way to begin the task of qualifying buyers – the subject covered in the pages that soon follow.

I also advocate that your notes on each prospect with whom you've spoken be organized and easy to find in your file. And support these buyer records with a follow-up system keyed to your calendar so you're reminded to contact the person three or four days later. Ask if the prospect has any questions and if they are interested in pursuing it further.

Remember that you're engaged in the dance, and that you're prepared to provide more information in return for some answers to your questions about what they are looking for, what kind of work experience and what is their price range.

Your prospect may have specific questions related to the facts provided on the blind profile and may want to know about information not covered, such as details of the financial performance, the number of hours you devote and your duties, the future of your industry and any problems you foresee in the business.

There also may be questions about how flexible you are in the price and terms, which may be a sign that the prospect lacks the financial ability to complete the deal. Or it may be an indication that you've got a prospect who wants to start negotiating before it has been established that he or she has a solid interest in buying the business.

A response I recommend for questions posed initially about your "flexibility" is to let the prospect know you would like to see a complete offer, and know about the financial ability and work experience of the person making the offer before commenting. You also can suggest that the person focus on one issue at a time. One comment I like is: "Don't you think it makes sense for you to learn more about the business and if you're interested in it, before we get into negotiating? My accountant thinks this is quite fairly priced. If you decide you want to own this business, you'd be hurting your chances of beating out other buyers, by trying to get a lower price or better terms before you've had a chance to find out what it is really worth to you."

Another way of responding to the question about your willingness to "deal" is with your own question about the buyer's ability. "Is the down payment more than you can handle?"

Some of the other questions you might encounter as you begin to qualify prospective buyers, and some strategies for participating in this dance will be covered in greater detail in the following chapter.

The Package

Our focus here is on that phase of the process when you provide more information, selectively, and recommend a meeting (suggest a coffee shop or other public place) so you and the prospect can learn more about the possibility of doing business with one another.

As the blind profile was the primary tool used to respond to initial inquiries and engage the interest of prospects, the package is the collection of information about your business which you will use to further the dialog with the prospect and take the relationship to the next step. Included in the package is a more extensive profile, identifying the company and giving a brief review of its financials. (See the business profile at the end of this chapter.) Copies of financial information (P & L and balance sheet for the current year to date and the past three years), your asset list (with an appraisal of equipment if possible), your lease and other agreements you need to conduct business, also belong in the package. Another item to include is any newspaper or magazine articles you can find which support your assertion that your company is in a growth industry or in a healthy and growing geographic area. And franchise businesses owners will want to include some of the promotional material produced by your franchisor.

A description of the ideal buyer is an excellent addition to your package.

What education, background and experience should someone have in order to be successful in the business? How much working capital? This inclusion is likely to provoke further interest in your offering on the part of buyers who have the requisite credentials. And it can provide an automatic screening function, making it less likely that you'll hear from – and have your time wasted by – people who are not qualified.

You may find that even before you send out, or hand out your package, that it is useful as a reference for responding to the questions posed by the prospective purchasers when you follow up after the initial contact. Tell the prospect you've got on the phone that you are reading from your documents, so you can explain things in more detail.

Then, your offer to present the entire package to the party, in person, brings you to the suggestion that you and the prospective buyer meet to exchange information.

And remember that it's never too soon to impress on prospects the importance of maintaining confidentiality about the offering. Some sellers think it's sufficient to mention it once, and get a signed non-disclosure agreement, then neglect to bring it up again, assuming the prospect got the message. I think you need to introduce early the idea that a buyer's respect for your confidentiality request is critically important to you. By repeating this theme and reminding buyers about it, you will lessen the chances of a leak during the marketing of your business.

Being the Bearer of Bad News

You'll notice, elsewhere in these pages, that I advocate being the source of any negative information that might be encountered by prospects who are learning about your business. An interested buyer will discover, during due diligence examination, any factors that are likely to impact the future of your company's sales or profits. Don't wait for that. Let prospects find out from you. By doing this, you'll earn the trust of buyers and you'll have a chance to explain negative information and put it in proper perspective. One seller whose retail business was at risk because of the "big box" competitor moving into the area, made sure to inform prospective buyers about this. Then he said he would help to craft an ad campaign for the buyer, emphasizing his company's service tradition and its other strengths, and pointing out the disadvantages of doing business with a large, nation-wide chain store, that had no real connection to the community.

Timing the release of less-than-positive information takes some careful thought. You don't want to discourage a prospective purchaser before he or she has a chance to become interested in your business. Many people, once they're enthused about something, will tolerate a certain amount of negative information. The same buyers learning this same information at the outset might have rejected the offering, because they hadn't yet developed an interest in it. On the other hand, you don't want to waste a lot of time with a seemingly motivated buyer who will pull out of the deal at the last minute, scared away when the bad news is finally revealed.

I advocate preparing a written disclosure stating the facts, and including your opinion about how the negative might be turned into a positive. The statement should be shown to the buyer as soon as you detect the person has a strong interest in the business.

Conclusion

The objective in this chapter has been to help the do-it-yourself business seller to get the word out about the offering, in a controlled manner, and then be in position to respond to questions and move the conversation along toward the next step. In the following chapter, we'll cover the process by which the prospective buyer learns more about the business and agrees to keep your secrets as well as revealing his or her financial ability, work history and general ability to be your buyer.

Throughout this process it is strongly recommended that you maintain an organized file of buyers containing complete notes about your contact with each. And hang onto those folders. I know of more than one occasion when a seller learned a deal in process would not go through, and went back to buyer information so as to contact other interested prospects and find someone else to purchase the business.

KEY POINTS FROM THIS CHAPTER

❖ *By following some of the suggestions offered in previous pages, you've had control over the early stages of the sales process. The uncertainty begins when you offer the business to the marketplace and wait to find out it there will be interest and positive reaction. Much of the chapter contains information to help you exert as much influence as possible on the process that follows.*

❖ *The interesting marketing problem you face is how to broadcast the availability of your business as widely as possible, still keeping it a secret from anyone whom you don't want to have the information. That includes employees, customers, vendors and competitors.*

❖ *The strategy for dealing with the marketing challenge is to conduct the process of marketing in phases, starting with initial introduction using a "blind profile" (the company is not identified). A later phase is to meet a prospective buyer and engage in the "dance" whereby each reveals a little information, then progressively more information, until it's determined either that you want to conduct negotiations with a transaction in mind, or that one or both of you don't want to do business.*

❖ *It can't be stressed enough how important the first 30 to 60 days of your campaign can be. If the initial offering of your business is mishandled, it can substantially increase the difficulty of finding the right buyer and ruin the likelihood of your getting a satisfactory deal in a short period of time. Don't lose good buyers because of lack of preparation or inattentiveness to their requests.*

❖ *A good advertising strategy, if you have the resources, is to run your business for sale ad in print as well as online media which cater to business buyers, such as **www.bizben.com** Don't skimp on advertising. It would be a shame not to get the best offer simply because there weren't enough qualified people aware of the availability of the business.*

❖ *It is suggested that newspaper classified advertising in California be focused on Sunday issues only, as the weekday ads don't seem to draw much reaction – probably because they're not read.*

❖ *Wherever your ads appear – print or electronic, or both – use words and phrases that are known to provoke interest. Emphasizing growing business, excellent income, good terms, good lease, well established, and some of the other virtues listed in the chapter will help to make that phone ring in response to your ads.*

❖ *With their database of qualified buyers, brokers are an important resource even if you don't have the business listed. Get your blind profile to brokers so they can introduce the business to their clients. Some brokers represent buyers only and are paid to look for businesses like yours. Others might want to arrange with you to pay a half of the commission if they produce the buyer for your business. And it might be worth it to get a good buyer at your price and terms.*

❖ *You can't make it too easy for interested buyers to get in touch with you. Get a dedicated phone line so interested buyers seeing your ads can contact you. Make sure your line is equipped to take messages if you aren't available. Follow up immediately.*

❖ *Keep track of which advertising is working best, and is not working, in the event you want to modify your advertising campaign.*

❖ *Sellers are advised to start a file for sale of the business and to include information about all the inquiries. You never know when having this information will come in handy. For example, if you settle on a buyer who, it turns out, cannot perform on the agreement, won't you be glad you still have the contact information for the number two candidate?*

❖ *Follow up with those who've made an inquiry about your business and attempt to qualify them as to interest, financial strength and general ability to own your business.*

❖ *A more extensive profile of the business is for use when you meet with prospects and obtain their non-disclosure agreement. This business profile gives identifying information regarding your company, an overview of financial performance and – with the inclusion of relevant documents – details about your hard assets and your agreements with landlord, employees, customers and others.*

❖ *A description of the ideal buyer is a good component for inclusion in the package of information about your business. It can be a "turn-on" for those who would have what it takes. And it will help to discourage unqualified people with whom you probably should not be spending time.*

❖ *Your disclosure of any negative factors that may affect your business, along with an explanation of how to deal with these problems, is a much better way to handle this kind of information than ignoring it and hoping buyers won't discover it. They will find out about it on their own, in most cases, and if you neglected to "manage" this news, you'll have little opportunity to put it into a context that can help soften the blow and keep the buyer on track.*

❖ *Samples of a blind profile and a business profile can be found at the end of the chapter to give you some ideas about information for inclusion in these documents.*

❖ *The following chapter focuses on qualifying prospective buyers and prepares you and the most interested prospects to negotiate for their purchase of the business.*

Manufacturer of Mechanical Devices used in Consumer Electronics

Long Established   Very Profitable   Business Growing

Established: **17 Years**		Location: **Santa Clara County (No. CA)**	
Owner Responsibility: **Mgmt/Sales**		Reason for Sale: **Moving from area**	
Number Employees: **Owner + 5 FT + 2 PT**		Lease Length: **6 yr + (2) 4 yr options**	
Ownership: **"S" Corp**		Hours Operation: **M - Thu: 6:30 am - 4:00 pm,** **Fri: 6:30 am - 12 noon**	

Performance: **$125,660 adjusted net profit on sales of $637,326 in most recently completed fiscal year**

Opportunity for buyer to cash in on growth of this industry with well-established company respected for the quality of its products sold to long-term "blue-chip" customers. Seller will train and introduce to clients and remain with Buyer to assist in smooth transition.

Asking Price: $ 350,000 (plus about $20,000 for inventory of parts and finished goods)

Terms: $ 140,000 cash down payment required
           100,000 independent financing available for qualified buyers
           110,000 seller carry back for 5 years
                  at 4.5% interest; mo. payment of $2,050.73
          ——————
          $ 350,000

Asset sale
Price includes: Machinery and Equipment: $143,000 at current book value
                Leasehold improvements: 30,000 at current book value
                Goodwill   140,000
                Covenant not to Compete   37,000 for five years
                Total $350,000

Other: To be delivered to Buyer free and clear of obligations and payables. Working capital requirement: $100,000 estimated for: purchase inventory of parts and finished goods ($20,000), various tax and other deposits required from new owner ($5,000), accounts receivable funding ($65,000), working capital ($10,000).

For additional Information: Call seller, Lou, at 650 555.1234

Offered for sale

Phlquex Manufacturing
6789 Standard Business Street
San Jose, CA

For added Information:

Owner, Lou: 650 555.1234

Overview:

Opportunity to benefit from growth of this industry with well-established company known for the quality of its products sold to long-term "blue chip" customers. Seller will train and introduce buyer to clients and remain with business for a few weeks to assist in smooth transition.

Business information:

Established: 1988
Owner Responsibility: Manage operations, conduct sales
Reason for Sale: Seller moving from area
Number of Employees: Owner + 5 full-time + 2 part-time
Size of facility: Office 700 sq. ft.; Manufacturing 3,300 sq ft.; Warehouse 2,400 sq ft.
Lease length: 6 years remaining + (2) 4 year options to renew at market rates
Hours of operation: Mon - Thur: 6:30 am to 4:00 pm, Fri: 6:30 am to 12 noon.

Financial Performance:

Year to Date (07/1/04-09/30/04)	P & L	Fiscal Year Ended 06/30/04	P & L	Fiscal Year Ended 6/30/03	P & L
Total Revenues	$ 173,672	Total Revenues	$ 637,326	Total Revenues	$ 586,977
Cost of sales	78,658	Cost of Sales	271,983	Cost of Sales	268,524
Gross Profit	95,014	Gross Profit	365,343	Gross Profit	318,453
Overhead	74,303	Overhead	293,962	Overhead	252,505
Net Income	20,711	Net Income	71,381	Net Income	65,948
Seller Add Backs	14,560	Seller Add Backs	54,379	Seller Add Backs	47,854
Total Adjusted Net Income	$ 35,271	Total Adjusted Net Income	$ 125,760	Total Adjusted Net Income	$ 113,802

Phlquex Manufacturing - Page 2.

Financial Condition:

Fiscal Year Ended 6/30/04	Balance Sheet
Assets	
Cash	$ 17,546
Machinery /Equip	137,706
Inventory parts	11,647
Finished goods	6,338
Vehicles	4,200
Accounts Rec.	84,392
Other, Deposits	618
Depreciation (accumulated)	(44,850)
Leasehold	30,000
Goodwill	50,000
Total	**$ 297,597**

Liabilities	
Accounts Payable	7,624
Long term debt (note to owner)	12,500
Total	**$ 20,124**

Equity	**$ 277,473**

Customers:

Include such firms as XYZ Corp and NOP International which incorporate the Phlquex Model II and Phlquex Model III in the manufacture of VCRs, Camcorders, and related consumer electronics items.

Purchase Terms:

Asking Price: $350,000 plus about $20,000 inventory of parts and finished goods
Terms: 140,000 cash down payment to seller
100,000 independent financing available
110,000 Seller carry back for 5 years at 4.5%; mo payments of $20,050.,73

Selling assets of corporation as follows:

Machinery & Equipment	$ 143,000	at book value
Leasehold Improvements	30,000	at book value
Goodwill	140,000	
Covenant not to Compete	37,000	for five years
Total	$ 350,000	

To be delivered to Buyer free and clear of obligations and payables. Working capital required, approximately $100,000 estimated for: Inventory of parts/finished goods ($20,000), tax and deposits required ($5,000), accounts receivables ($65,000), working capital ($10,000).

Seller to be available to train for three months after close of escrow.

See attached for recent newspaper articles about the growth in the industry.

CHAPTER TEN

QUALIFYING BUYERS: A CRITICAL STEP

If the preparation, both of your company and your selling package, is the most important thing you can do when offering your small California business for sale, the next most important – and it runs a close second – is to be sure that you are working only with buyer prospects who are qualified to do business with you.

Perhaps this seems like a requirement so obvious that it doesn't need to be mentioned. Yet it's actually quite easy to get so caught up in the selling process-answering questions, conducting tours of the facility, providing information – that you neglect to verify that the person you're working with actually has the ability to move forward on a purchase of your business if, in fact, the prospect wants to do so.

Even the most experienced sales people run the risk of engaging in wishful thinking from time to time. They come to like a certain "buyer" and believe that the person, who has been so cooperative and easy to work with, is going to be able to perform when it comes time to put up the money and sign on the dotted line.

Because your time is too valuable to waste with unqualified buyers, sellers are reminded of the importance that you should place on finding out for certain, early in the interactions with a prospect, that the person is a real buyer. Yes, it is sometimes difficult to coax the information you need out of someone who's inquiring about your offering. And you do risk chasing away a good, qualified buyer by insisting on getting answers to your questions before the person is ready to share. But it's worth the risk so as to avoid the wasted time and the frustration that come from trying to make a sale to someone who can't buy.

How Business Brokers Walk the Tightrope

It's useful for sellers, whether or not you are experienced at qualifying prospective customers in your business, to take a lesson from skilled business brokers who are good at managing this step in the process. One broker describes the art of qualifying buyers as "walking the tightrope."

"If you push too hard for information," he explains, "the prospect can feel boxed in and surrounded. The only escape is to run from you. And if that was a good buyer who got away – well, you just lost."

But the alternative, he points out, is to fail to ask the important questions early in the conversation: "If you don't learn what you need to know, you might find out you're just being led down the garden path. There are plenty of sweet sentiments along your way. But no sale. It's another way to lose."

This broker recommends adopting a helpful attitude, with a willingness to answer questions and do what you can, so people understand what you have to offer. But then temper your helpfulness with an insistence on getting the cooperation of the other party.

He says: "It's fine to treat a prospective buyer for your business the way you do the customers who you deal with on a daily basis. They get your attention; your energy is there to provide service.

"But don't cross the line on the side of being overly accommodating without expecting some consideration in return."

Another broker explains that good sales people in most any industry attempt to – in her words – "orchestrate the interaction as much as possible.

"You can't really control another person," she says. "In fact, that's not something you want to do. It's not healthy for people to relate to each other that way. And it's not good business."

She continues: "But you do want to take the initiative, if you can. You can set the agenda and make sure your objectives are clearly on the table. You get more accomplished that way, than if you just shake hands with the prospective buyer and talk about the weather to break the ice and then hope for the best."

Here are example conversation openers that will give you ideas about setting the tone in a meeting with a prospective buyer so that the dance referred to in the previous chapter is at least conducted according to your rhythm. Consider these ideas and think about how you can adapt one or more of these approaches to your style and personality.

Example One

I think it would use your time efficiently, and also mine, if we exchange some information. Then you can consider whether you are interested in investigating my business further and I can evaluate whether I think you'd make a suitable buyer.

I'd like to go over the basic information about the business and I have a package to give you to study so you can determine if you might want to buy the business. At the same time, I want to know more about you, I am interested in learning the same kind of information about you that I'm giving you about the business.

I'd like to understand a bit about your background, and I want to know about your financial situation: how much cash you have to work with and if you have arranged for added financing to help you make a purchase. I also want to know if you have good credit. That's in case we agree on a deal for the business that includes me carrying back some of the purchase price with a promissory note.

Does this seem fair?

I have a non-disclosure form here for you to agree to. And if you want me to acknowledge in writing that I will not share any information about your personal and financial situation except with my business advisors, I'll be glad to do that.

(An example form is available at bizben.com. Select Forms page and find Non-Disclosure & Confidentiality Agreement. Note where the business name is inserted. Provide the form with space for you to insert your business name once the buyer has reviewed and signed the form. It also calls for your signature and each of you should get a copy.)

Example Two

When we spoke and I sent you a (blind) profile on the business, I also included a non-disclosure form. I'd like to get that back from you with your approval of it (signed), and then we can proceed with me giving you more information about the business and answering your questions.

Did you bring the form? If not, I have another one here. I'm sure you understand how important it is that the information I'm about to give you is treated with the strictest confidentiality.

I also sent you a blank financial statement form. Did you get a chance to complete that? I'm willing to disclose to you some very private data about my business. It's important you know these things so that you can decide if this business is for you. At the same time, I think it's only fair that I understand about your background and financial ability. And I will treat any information you give me with the same respect for confidentiality that you treat the information I give you.

If you didn't bring your financial statement I have another blank here. I realize you don't have your personal records with you so you may not have all the details at your disposal. But just fill it out to the best of your ability, and please put your signature at the bottom. I'll give you a few minutes to go ahead and do that, and then we can talk about the business.

Example Three

As you can probably imagine, I have had a number of calls in response to my advertising. The fact is, there just are not that many good businesses available and at reasonable terms. So a lot of people have contacted me and are interested in learning more.

I'm pleased to answer all of your questions as well as I can, and to give you as much information as you need, so you can decide if this business is of interest. And in order to do that, I just need to verify that you are one of the people I've heard from who would be a suitable buyer – if you're interested.

So if you can answer a few questions for me, that'll help us move forward in this process.

Okay?

In the interests of respecting your time, and mine, I put a couple of forms in the mail to you – a non-disclosure agreement and a financial statement. Why don't we start with those?

These ideas originate from experienced sales professionals who understand that no one solution is applicable to every situation. And that some situations – and some people – can be particularly difficult to manage.

Certainly you're correct if you've concluded that prospective buyers for your business aren't likely to fall in line with everything you suggest at every occasion. The intent in offering these phrases (in show business they would be called opening lines) is not to give you all the tools you need to dominate the conversation. That's not realistic. But they will have served their purpose if they provoke some ideas about how you might take the initiative and press for your objectives in meetings with prospective buyers.

The point of view I'd like to share with you is a perspective meant for sellers who have difficulty walking that tightrope mentioned a bit earlier. If your habit is to give customers the upper hand in negotiations or in disputes, the concept for you to take away from these paragraphs is that any prospective buyers for your business owe you as much respect as you owe them. They need to be willing to accommodate your needs – for confidentiality and for facts about their qualifications – if you are to be expected to answer their questions and provide the information they request.

And for sellers who are quick to assume that your buyer candidates should be dismissed, disregarded and distrusted – until they prove otherwise – these brief samples of dialogue are meant to demonstrate another approach you can take. If you can use it to get a prospect to participate in the dance, you can move forward in the process of mutual discovery, without the fear that you are giving everything away for free.

In either event, sellers are encouraged to think about these suggested approaches and consider how you might modify them so they are consistent with the way you tend to work and communicate with others.

Some Questions to Ask

I know brokers who have a list of qualifying questions and when they ask the prospective buyers for information they merely go down the page, from 1 through 25, recording every answer. It's good that they're careful not to miss anything when qualifying prospective buyers, but I like to be a little more spontaneous than that when talking to another person. It's also good to build a rapport. And that's easier to do when your interaction is more like conversation rather than taking a poll. Whatever your style, here are some questions for which you should have answers from prospective buyers who want to move forward and learn about your business.

First the questions calling for definitive answers – what I consider the quantitative evaluation. Note that this is the kind of questioning you can use to give your buyer a passing or failing grade. And the "right" answers are provided.

- Have you been looking for a business for awhile? (If less than six months, the prospect is still on the steep learning curve as to what's available and may not have a realistic picture of the market. If more than two years, this perfectionist is unlikely to find anything to buy without changing his/her requirements.)

- Do you know the kind of business you're looking for? (A "yes or "I have a general idea" is the answer you want. If the person claims to be "open to anything" it could be a sign of a buyer still not focused.)

- Have you owned a business before? (Many serious and qualified buyers have not yet taken the plunge so the lack of this background should not be reason to shut them out of contention. But someone who's been an owner is more likely to speak your language.)

- Have you got experience managing people? (If you have employees, it's best to get a "yes" to this question. Buyers without this experience may be in over their heads trying to run your company.)

- Have you made an offer on a business before? (The "yes" answer here tells you that your prospect is probably serious. Besides, having been involved in one or more prior offers, the prospect is probably getting an education in the realities of the market.)

- How much cash do you have to work with? (The right answer is, of course, whatever is the amount of cash necessary to make the down payment on your offering and still have enough remaining for working capital.)

- Have you made arrangements to get financing to help with a purchase? (The prospect should get double points for a "yes" answer. It demonstrates the prospect is serious and is planning ahead. It also means the person may be able to get the funds needed to take over your business.)

- Do you understand why it's so important to me to keep this process confidential? (Expect a "yes" answer and be worried if you don't get it. One reason to ask the question is to remind the prospect of how critical it is to you that the proprietary information you're sharing is not disclosed to others.)

- Have you got good credit? (Naturally, a prospect with a perfect credit history is preferable to one whose credit report sinks like the Titanic. But a business buyer with a less than pristine credit record may have a good explanation and should be given the benefit of the doubt. At least the answer "not perfect" is probably an honest one.)

Mixed in with these, should be a few qualitative questions. These are more open-ended, calling for some description on the part of the person being qualified. A good way to interpret these answers is to look at body language and try to guess what's on the buyer's mind as well as what comes out of his or her mouth. And depending on the answers, and the impression you get of the person while he or she is answering, you may decide to alter the "score" they got when responding to the questions of the first type.

A few suggested qualitative questions are:

- If you've made offers on another business – or other businesses – what happened? Did you make a purchase? If not, why not?

- Why do you want to own your own business?

- Tell me something about your working background?

- Do you want to be a passive owner or do you expect to be active in your business?

These questions – both the quantitative and qualitative questions – are among the most important ones to ask. And reviewing this list will probably help you to come up with others to pose to a prospective buyer who is looking at your small California business. For a sample form to use when interviewing and qualifying buyers, go to the Confidential Buyer Profile Form at **www.bizben.com/pdf/Confidential_Buyer_Profile_Form.pdf**

How to Make the Most of Your Meeting with Buyer Prospects

Speaking of asking questions, if you've given any thought to this process while reading about it, you may have questions of your own about how to successfully conduct the qualifying of buyer prospects. Here are a few insights.

Be clear about your objective

During your initial meeting with a prospective buyer, it's very helpful to keep in mind exactly what you are trying to achieve. Don't be a business owner who thinks the sale has to be made at the first session. That agenda will confuse you and frighten the buyer.

Instead, the three useful things to accomplish at this point are: 1. Give the buyer enough information about the business so that he or she can determine if interested. That should be easy to do if you have a well-prepared package to hand over. You can quickly review the material and answer any questions to complete the presentation. 2. Find out if the buyer is qualified to buy your business. The answers to your qualifying questions will give you some useful clues if you don't know for sure. And remember to take the pulse of your instincts. Ask yourself if this person is someone with whom you can do business; and someone who's likely to be successful as owner of your enterprise. 3. Set the stage for what comes next. It's a mistake to leave things up in the air. You don't want the prospective buyer to "get back to you when I get a chance." Agree on a date – at least two days and no more than a week forward – to speak again about whether the buyer wants to tour the facility and get more information. Your prospect needs, and should have a few days to digest the information and determine if your business warrants further investigation. But don't leave it open ended.

I've learned that delays are like a deadly disease that kills deals. Instill a sense of urgency in your buyers, making sure they understand it's important to you for discussions or negotiations to keep moving forward at a steady pace.

Non-disclosure/Confidentiality Agreement

This is the buyer prospect's written promise that whatever he or she learns about your business, including the fact that it is for sale, as a result of the interaction with you, will not be disclosed to any other party other than the buyer's immediate advisors. The legal community is not in unanimous agreement about the effectiveness or enforceability of these agreements. However some form of non-disclosure contract is used in virtually all introductions by business brokers and agents throughout California. For the most part it is considered a useful tool for at least putting the buyer on notice about the seller's requirements regarding confidentiality. In extreme examples of violation of this agreement, a buyer may be liable to you for any damages you suffered because of his or her actions.

Sellers are advised to decline giving information to prospective buyers without first obtaining a signature on the non-disclosure document. While a small percentage of buyer's refuse when asked to do so – usually trying to get an upper hand in the event of later negotiations – most prospective purchasers for small California businesses are willing to comply with this request.

Is he or she telling the truth?

Once you obtain the non-disclosure promise, it's very useful to get a financial statement. And it doesn't hurt to ask the buyer to obtain a letter from an officer at his or her bank that confirms the buyer's representations to you about cash on hand and assets.

Someone reluctant to be forthcoming with the facts you require, or unwilling to provide some proof to back up claims, may have something to hide. Repeating what I noted a little earlier in this chapter: If you have furnished the prospect with details about the business, or are about to do so, you have every right to expect the person to disclose the details of their background and their financial ability, as it pertains to the purchase of your business. If they don't want to cooperate, I feel they've proved themselves unqualified to buy your business.

If the person appears to be telling the truth, but is not, you will find out about it eventually – you hope sooner rather than later. I'm a strong advocate for taking back-up offers, even if you have a ratified contract with a buyer who is conducting a due diligence examination.

One reason to encourage back-up offers, even when you are in contract with someone who is now conducting due diligence examination, is to keep the "working" buyer moving forward. And make sure the buyer understands that you intend to have alternative buyers to work with if he or she proves unable to complete the deal as agreed. One strategy of buyers who don't provide accurate details about their financial ability, involves getting you to renegotiate the deal in their favor, once it is discovered they haven't the ability to perform according to the agreement. If such a buyer knows you're prepared to sell to someone else, if necessary, it may discourage this kind of dishonesty.

Keep your notes/folders up to date

Remember the file mentioned in the previous chapter – the one with folders containing all the information pertaining to the sale of your small California business? Make sure the buyer folder is current so that you can refer to facts given to you by prospective buyers in case there is a discrepancy. And in this or an adjacent folder, you should have names and contact information for other buyers to stay in touch with in the event the "working" deal begins to go bad – either because the buyer doesn't want to move forward or because you learn the new owner candidate was less than honest at the point where you were qualifying buyers.

What if the Buyer Doesn't Appear Qualified?

Do you know how to say "no?" Whether your tendency is to be diplomatic or blunt, it is important that you cut off discussion as soon as possible, after you've satisfied yourself that this prospect is not the buyer you want for your business. Perhaps you've reached this conclusion because you can't get agreement on signing the non-disclosure document. Maybe the person is unable or unwilling to give you satisfactory financial information, or the information provided reveals their inability to handle the purchase.

And it may be your gut reaction that tells you that time spent with the person will be wasted.

In any event, remember that you are a buyer also. You have to "buy" this buyer candidate as the one you might have a deal with – the individual who might replace you as owner of your business. The buyer has a right to decline to proceed if he or she doesn't want to buy your business. And you have the same right, if you don't consider the person qualified.

If your answer to the prospect is "no," make that clear as soon as possible. Then move on to the next prospect.

Conclusion

The intent in this chapter is to offer some insight into the process of qualifying prospective buyers for your small California business, and to provide some ideas about how to handle this important step. Without qualified buyers to work with, your efforts to sell your business are wasted. And unless buyers are correctly qualified as to work background and financial ability, there is no way to determine with certainty if anyone in the audience for whom you are presenting your business, has the capacity to join you in a transaction. As difficult as it might be for some sellers to qualify buyers before working with them, and to say "no" to those who don't qualify, it is absolutely critical that these steps are followed carefully if an owner is to achieve a successful sale of his or her business.

KEY POINTS FROM THIS CHAPTER

❖ *Properly qualifying prospective buyers is among the most important things a seller can do in the process of marketing a small California business.*

❖ *One broker describes the art of qualifying buyers as "walking the tightrope." Pushing too hard for information can chase a buyer away, while neglecting to get the information you need can result in wasting a lot of time with unqualified people.*

❖ *Another broker recommends that a seller meeting with a prospective buyer should attempt to "orchestrate the interaction as much as possible." That is done by taking the initiative and setting the agenda.*

❖ *Suggested approaches a seller can take to gain some control in a buyer qualifying meeting include: "I think it would use your time efficiently if we exchange information," "I'm willing to disclose information to you ... at the same time I think it's only fair that I understand about your background and financial ability," and "I'm pleased to answer all of your questions ... just need to verify you're one of the people who would be a suitable buyer."*

❖ *Sellers who are so accustomed to providing service to customers that they're reluctant to demand financial and other personal information, should understand that buyers need to be just as accommodating as sellers are in the disclosure of information.*

❖ *Some qualifying questions to ask buyers are quantitative, requiring definitive answers. Questions of a more qualitative nature give further insight into the buyer's probable ability to complete a deal.*

❖ *Don't attempt to make a sale on an initial meeting with a buyer. Rather, the time is well spent if you can: 1. Provide the buyer with solid information about your business, 2. Find out if the buyer is qualified, and 3. Set the stage for follow up, with a definite date to further discuss a possible deal.*

❖ *Written information from a buyer, such as financial statement and banker letter, can help add credibility to a buyer's verbal assertions. Sellers are encouraged to obtain it.*

❖ The Buyer's signature on a Non-disclosure/Confidentiality Agreement, early in the process, helps to prevent "leaks" of proprietary information about the seller's business, and puts the buyers on notice that they will be required to maintain confidentiality during their investigation of the offering. At this web address: **www.bizben.com/selling-buying-business-forms.php**, you can obtain and download a Non-disclosure/Confidentiality Agreement form.

❖ It's important to keep a file in which you maintain buyer information and also names and contact data for other buyers who might be willing to provide back-up offers if a "working" buyer can't perform. Encouraging back ups is a good strategy to keep your buyer moving forward.

❖ Delays kill deals. Make sure all buyer prospects understand that you consider it important for discussions and negotiations to move forward at a steady pace.

❖ When encountering buyers who aren't qualified, it helps if you know how to say "no." Whether your style is diplomatic or blunt, cut off discussion with the wrong buyer as soon as possible, so you can be free to deal with qualified buyers.

CHAPTER ELEVEN

SOLICITING OFFERS

Some professional sales people can't wait till they get through their presentation and answer all the questions and objections so they can arrive at their favorite part – asking for the order. Others will do most anything to avoid the moment of truth, forcing themselves to work on closing the sale because they have to in order to complete the job. But they dislike it because they fear hearing a "no," and having it stir up feelings of inadequacy and the experience of getting rejected.

Whether or not you're comfortable with this critical part of the sale process, it'll be useful for you to have knowledge about the point where the buyer is asked to make a commitment, and to understand how to make that happen. If necessary, you'll be prepared to move from discussion with a prospective buyer to a written contract so you can sell your business.

And you may not require this skill at all. If your most interested buyers like what they see, you may find that closing the sale is no more complicated than simply smiling and saying "thank you" when one or more of them comes forward with a written offer to purchase along with a deposit check made out to an escrow company to get the transaction started.

But even a motivated buyer can use a little prodding sometimes. After all, as excited as someone might be about your company – and the idea of owning it – that little voice of caution may be reminding the buyer about all the many reasons he or she should hold off and not take this plunge. A touch of encouragement may be all that's required to get things moving forward. And if you've taken on the job of selling your own business, then it's your responsibility to give that imperceptible push to get the buyer's commitment.

But how to do it?

A Suggested Protocol

As a do-it-yourself seller, you lose the benefit of distance that a third party, such as a business broker, can use to their advantage in getting negotiations started. Part of the discussion between a broker and buyer at this point has to do with how they can construct an offer that will meet the buyer's needs and also appeal to the seller. In that conversation the broker goes over the particulars – price and terms – and works out an offer for the buyer to sign. Meanwhile you, the seller, are somewhere else waiting to see if you are going to get a proposal and wondering what it might be.

Now take the broker out of the equation and it's just you and the buyer. So, the dynamics are drastically different. You can't very well speculate with the buyer about what the seller may want to see – the seller is you and you know very well what it'll take to buy your business. But you're not about to reveal your bottom line at this point.

This awkward situation demonstrates one of the times when a broker comes in very handy. But there are ways you can deal with this matter if you can just take yourself out of the picture. You can suggest that the buyer prepare an offer – when he or she is ready – then mail it to you or drop it off at your office (when no employees are present) or at the office of your attorney or accountant. Explain that you're assuming the offer will match up with your asking price and terms and you'll agree to move forward. And let the buyer know that if there is any thinking and deciding to do on your part – in other words if the offer won't match every part of your request – you ought to be given a few days to review and consider what's proposed before having to accept or counter offer.

And if you can get an attorney or a broker (for a simple fee) to intervene in this particular circumstance, it may make a difficult situation much easier for the buyer. After all, if you've been talking to one another for awhile, the buyer may not want to confront you directly with a set of terms that don't meet yours. A third party helps to cushion this anxiety-producing situation.

And here are some of the tools used by business broker pros, not to mention professionals in most any field of sales, to get an interested prospect to take action toward becoming a buyer.

The Hammer

One of my associates tells the story of a business broker who gained a reputation as the "Hammer" because he was so direct with clients. It's not that he didn't know how to subtly build a case for a proposed deal until the buyer finally came to the conclusion that some kind of commitment would be in order. The *Hammer* simply didn't have the patience. He wanted to get a deal started whenever talking to a prospect. If somebody with whom he was working couldn't see the benefits of moving forward, the Hammer would just tell the person "call me when you're ready to make a decision." Then he'd find someone else on whom he could apply this tactic.

The *Hammer's* assumption was always that the prospect was ready to make an offer. Whenever someone voiced some questions, the *Hammer* would say: "Okay, I'll answer your questions. If you are satisfied with the answers, then are you going to make an offer?"

It's not surprising that some people objected to this treatment. In fact, there were times when the *Hammer* was told to "back off." And there were complaints to the head of the brokerage about this conduct. And yet the *Hammer* was among the top producers for the company, selling businesses and closing deals with regularity. And I think this demonstrates that although he did aggravate and annoy a few people, there is some merit to the very direct selling style.

I'm not advocating that sellers all should push their buyers for a decision by pounding away like the *Hammer*. But in your toolkit of methods for getting commitments, when you feel it's time to stop discussing and start negotiating, it might be useful to know about this approach.

If you're dealing with someone who seems interested in buying your company but has not volunteered to submit an offer, even after several conversations, and with all of his or her major questions answered, maybe you can take a lesson from the *Hammer*. You can come right out and ask the individual: "Why don't you make an offer?" or "Are you prepared to make an offer?"

Whether or not that tactic gets the prospect to make a decision – and regardless of what the decision might be – you will have a better idea of where this person stands on the notion of buying your business. And if the prospect is not ready to move forward, it's best you know that so you can focus time and energy on other prospects.

Remember that a certain percentage of buyers for a business – or buyers of anything, for that matter – find it difficult to make a commitment. They worry about the risks involved and fear doing most anything they might later regret.

That's why there's an important place in business for professional sales people who know how to help others overcome their innate sales resistance and move forward. Were it not for business professionals introducing a sense of urgency into the buying process for their customers, many, if not most companies would collapse, and so would our economy.

One frequently used tool to make this happen is the *hammer*.

The Tweezers

Of course the *hammer* doesn't work with everyone. What about people who resent being pressured – prospects who think that a forceful salesperson has to behave that way in order to get people to buy inferior products or services?

As we summarized the methods of aggressive and direct selling with the description of the *hammer*, we can apply the term, the "tweezers", to a more subtle selling style – that of extracting little commitments from a buyer, one-by-one, in order to get the person to take action.

When this tool is used to move a prospective business buyer forward, the attention is focused on discrete issues within the overall objective of preparing an offer.

For example, one approach might be: "Is this lease satisfactory to you?" And if the response to this is in the affirmative, the follow up is: "Well then, will we require that the seller assign the lease to you, when we start putting your offer together?"

The strategy here, of course, is to identify each and every single part of what will be the whole – that is – the offer. The lease terms, the length of training, the duration of the covenant not to compete, and of course the price to be offered, the down payment proposed, terms of seller financing and other issues of concern to the buyer are gently pulled out, one at a time, as with a pair of *tweezers*, until there's nothing left to discuss besides putting this all together in a contract.

The Yardstick

The *tweezers* method of bringing a buyer to the point of commitment is similar to what is called the "yardstick". That strategy is a favorite of sales people who want to know if their prospect is a buyer without asking the question directly, for fear of seeming too pushy, and losing the prospect's confidence.

Yardstick questions often begin with the phrase "If you were," as in: "If you were to make an offer on this business, what is the price you think would work for you?" Or "If you were to meet the seller's price, how much down payment do you think you'd want to go in with?"

Any answer provoked by this line of questioning is helpful in letting the sales person know where to place the buyer on the spectrum of readiness that spans the distance from the initial introduction to "let's make a deal."

The *yardstick* and its cousin, the *tweezers*, are sales methods that recognize the delicate balance in the relationship between a sales person and prospect. Each needs the other and yet they have fears about the interaction. The person with the money to spend – on a business, a car, a garment or any other of millions of products and services available in the marketplace – is fearful about being "talked into" doing something that will prove to be detrimental rather than beneficial.

And the sales person fears spending time and effort introducing and explaining an idea that can benefit the prospect, without achieving a sale. For the commissioned sales professional, such as a business broker, the failure to make a deal has a dollar value –

the amount that would have been earned had things turned out differently. This value can also be thought of as the sales commission that was lost by not having spent that time with someone else, a different prospect who might have been prepared to buy.

Being fearful then, the two engage in a way that allows them to keep communicating, to continue learning about one another, and to move closer to what each wants to get out of this relationship. The interaction might end prematurely were it not for the sales person using the *yardstick*.

Imagine how it would affect the amount of service, the kind of help you receive from a sales person if you were to say: "Just tell me all the information you have on this subject and answer all my questions, and maybe I'll let you know – when I'm good and ready – whether I'm interested in making a purchase. And maybe that's when I'll reveal whether I'm willing to make a fair offer, or I'm planning to try and get something for nothing with a low-ball price or a no-down payment deal."

And as a sales person, you can likely picture what would happen to the rapport with your prospect if you said: "I'd just as soon not go over this information with you until you tell me if you're planning to make an offer at, or near asking price and terms."

The *yardstick* is managed by the sales person but it's a useful mechanism for both parties in this interaction, allowing them to balance out their somewhat mutual and also contradictory interests.

The Vise

A blending of the forcefulness of the *hammer* and the subtleties of the *tweezers* and the *yardstick*, is the "vise". It's a sales method that is readily applicable to the process of selling small California businesses – particularly those businesses that generate broad appeal.

"I don't mean to pressure you, but …" is something a sales person might say as the *vise* is tightened.

The statement proceeds: "… there are other people looking at this profitable company. If we don't get a bid in right away, you might lose it."

And then this powerful thought can be introduced to maximize the effect of the *vise*: "I'd hate to think we have this opportunity to put in an offer, but fail to do it. I hope that later on you won't say: 'I should have bought that business when I had the chance.'"

If the prospect is unconcerned with this disguised threat, it could be that he or she doesn't have enough interest in the business to take action. In that event, the sales person derives a *yardstick* benefit from the *vise*, and now can focus on other opportunities which the prospect might like more. But if there is intense interest in the business being discussed, the *vise* might be just the tool to get the prospect moving on it.

What to Include With an Offer

In addition to the price and seller finance terms that are spelled out in a buyer's offer to purchase a small California business, there should be a list of what the buyer wants as part of the deal. Such a list can be attached to the offer as an exhibit, or if there are few capital assets, the items can be mentioned right in the offer.

The exact value of parts, materials and finished goods that will be in the warehouse and on the books at close of escrow may not be known when the offer is made. Frequently, this quandary is addressed by specifying an inventory value, measured by its cost, which is to be included for the price. As part of this understanding, a careful physical inventory will be taken at close of escrow, and the business sales price will be adjusted up or down, depending on how the final valuation compares with the amount specified in the contract.

For example, if the books of a manufacturing company show that the business owns $10,000 of components at cost (what was paid for them) and $15,000 of finished goods at cost (including what was paid for components and the labor cost to have them assembled into saleable products) the total of $25,000 could be the expected amount of inventory to change hands when the business transfers. If the actual inventory figure is, for example, $28,000, when the deal closes and the count is conducted, the $3,000 difference would be added to the sales price. And visa versa: a $21,000 inventory would warrant subtraction of $4,000 from the agreed on price.

An alternative way to treat this is for the offer to specify a price for the business that does not include the inventory. Then, when the inventory is taken, directly prior to completing the transaction, the dollar value of components and finished goods would be paid for in addition to the purchase price.

Other elements that ordinarily are included in an offer are:

Allocation of purchase price: This is the amount of money applied to each of the assets involved in the deal, with the sum of these values equal to the selling price. This part of a transaction has tax implications for both parties and should be discussed with tax advisors prior to their agreement. The subject of allocation will be treated in more detail in a subsequent chapter.

Treatment of the lease: Will the buyer accept the existing lease, with the understanding that it must be transferable to buyer according to present terms and conditions? Does the buyer expect a new lease, and what are the required terms? These questions are addressed in the offer.

Duration of the seller's covenant not to compete and training agreement: The covenant is usually expressed in years, and usually is ascribed a dollar value in the allocation of purchase price. The training usually is part of the good will and is not treated as a separate asset, although it could be if the parties to the deal so specify. The length of the seller's training commitment typically ranges from a few days to several weeks.

Due Diligence: This is the buyer's right to examine records, documents and other information related to the business to determine whether the company functions and profits as was represented. Until the seller and buyer have an agreement for transfer of the business, it wouldn't be appropriate for the buyer to delve into the seller's proprietary information about the company. But having worked out an agreeable plan with the seller to take over the company, the buyer has earned the right to evaluate the details of operations, and even to share them with advisors, such as accountants, lawyers and tax specialists. During the due diligence period, the buyer can opt out of the deal at any time, if not satisfied with evaluation of the company, or if informed of possible future problems with the business.

The specific acts or approvals of other parties required: In addition to a franchisor, or the landlord, there may be outside lenders (if a loan assumption is part of the deal), licensing and/or taxing authorities (to cover any permits or licenses required), and others whose cooperation is required by the buyer before the business deal can be finalized in such a way that meets the buyer's requirements.

The timelines required: The seller has a specific number of days in which to accept or respond to the offer in order for it to remain alive. The buyer has a specified amount of time also, to conduct and complete the due diligence process, gain approval for any outside financing needed, and resolve any other matters which are conditions of proceeding with the deal. It's recommended that the due diligence period be set at from seven to ten business days. If one or both fail to meet these written time commitments – absent a later agreement by the parties for a time extension – the deal is considered to have become null and void when the first unmet deadline is reached. It's not uncommon, however, for parties to keep working toward a deal, even if some needed item remains unfinished past its deadline. The continued involvement of both parties and their intention to perform under the agreement keeps their deal alive and valid.

Warranties and representations: Both buyer and seller agree to various provisions in an offer that confirm such things as their legal capacity to do business and the truth of statements they've made to each other.

Follow up required: An escrow holder is usually mentioned and the buyer's deposit check, made out to escrow is frequently included, to demonstrate good intention. The buyer notes any other things that have to take place, such as the satisfactory conclusion of the due diligence examination, before the escrow can be opened. Then compliance with escrow instructions can be detailed or mentioned and a targeted date for concluding the deal is specified.

There may be other requirement that a buyer wishes to include in an offer but most transactions can be concluded based on satisfactory outcome and agreement on these points noted for inclusion in the offer. Please see the sample business sales contract to note what items are included. **Go to www.bizben.com/selling-buying-business-forms.php**

Asset vs. Stock Deal

One additional part of the offer that should be mentioned pertains to businesses owned by corporations – not just large corporations, but small, individually held corporations. That part is the declaration of whether the deal will be for corporate assets or corporate stock. The assumption used in describing the sale of assets, is that the seller, whether an individual or corporation, is going to transfer to the buyer the specified and separate assets of the business. Each is given a value in the allocation, and the buyer is then free to organize these assets as he or she sees fit. Meanwhile, the seller keeps the corporation. This is the form of sale of some 90% of small California corporations, and will represent the model for how a business is sold in our discussions.

The less common way to sell small California businesses (accounting for only one in ten transactions), is for the individual who owns a corporation – which, in turn, owns the subject business – to sell the stock in that corporation. In that event, the buyer becomes a new shareholder, usually the majority holder, and the corporate assets are considered to be transferred all at once, within the corporate shell, and at the values listed in the corporation's balance sheet.

One analogy that brokers use to explain this difference is that of a toy box. The assets are the toys, the corporation is the box. In the asset sale, the seller takes the toys out of the box and stacks them up for the buyer to admire, evaluate and purchase. In that stack, of course, is the right to own and conduct the business. The corporate sale, however, can be described as the sale of the box – its value agreed on between the parties – with all its contents included.

Whether buyer and seller agree on an asset or a stock sale depends largely on their individual tax and financial situations. That's why we repeatedly advise clients to check with their tax advisors to determine what is in their best interests. Some ideas about tax consequences for sellers are treated in a subsequent chapter.

And there's a serious matter of liability that makes an asset purchase a preferable approach for most buyers. That's because the individual items purchased as assets come without any debt or encumbrance about which the buyer is not informed or has not accepted. When the buyer takes over corporate stock, however, there is exposure to any liens or liabilities the corporation may have incurred prior to close of the transaction. The buyer becomes responsible for these problems because they stay with the corporation.

As noted in an earlier chapter, there may be occasions when the buyer prefers to acquire the stock. Such an example is when permits, licenses or other privileges owned by the corporation cannot readily be transferred from party to party. The buyer might buy the corporation by purchasing its stock, in order to gain its favorable lease, customer agreements or other corporate assets.

Conclusion

In order to successfully sell your business, it's imperative that you keep the momentum going with any interested buyer. That's easy to do in the early stages when the conversation is informal and you and prospects are getting acquainted. But you'll never get a deal if one or more of these people don't declare their intention to buy and do so in writing.

How to get that to occur, if the prospect doesn't take the initiative, is discussed with the emphasis on tools used by professional sales people to close deals. They include the hammer, the tweezers, the yardstick and the vise. And a strategy is suggested for dealing with the challenge presented you when there is no third party to act as go between for you and an interested buyer.

The key components of an offer are reviewed and sellers are given a bit of insight into the issues involved in deciding, when a corporation is actual owner of the business, whether to sell the assets of the business or the corporate stock.

KEY POINTS FROM THIS CHAPTER

❖ *Even a motivated buyer can use a little encouragement sometimes to step forward on a deal. Sellers who are handling the marketing of their own company have the responsibility for "closing" the sale.*

❖ *Without the benefit of a third party between you and a buyer, it's your job to somehow manage the sometimes awkward task of soliciting offers. One suggestion is to have the buyer prepare their offer and mail it, or drop it off at your office (when no employees are present) or at the office of your accountant or attorney.*

❖ *In order to actually get a prospect to make an offer it sometimes is necessary to use tools familiar to professional sales people. One such tool is the hammer (named for a business broker I know of who had that nickname). The hammer technique involves being direct and forceful. Using this tool you would simply tell, or ask, a prospect to make an offer.*

❖ *Since the hammer doesn't work with everyone, an alternative method of closing is the tweezers – a more subtle selling style in which you identify each and every single part of the whole – the offer – and get the buyer to make a choice, one by one of what to include.*

❖ *Similar to the tweezers is the yardstick, a way of measuring the readiness of a prospect to do business. Yardstick questions usually begin: "If you were to move forward with an offer on this deal, how would you want to... (fill in the blank)?*

❖ *The vise is another closing tool mentioned. Its function is to let the prospect know that if there is too much hesitation, he or she runs the risk of losing what they want.*

❖ *When it comes time to put an offer together, your buyer should include a list of what is expected to be part of the purchase.*

❖ *Inventory can be either included in the purchase price or added on after a final count of parts and other inventory items, at close of escrow.*

❖ *Other parts of the purchase agreement should include allocation of price, treatment of the lease and the terms of your covenant not to compete and your training agreement.*

❖ *Also included in an offer are the buyer's requirements about specific acts or approvals by other parties: lender, landlord, taxing authority, licensing agency, franchisor and any others whose cooperation is needed for the buyer to be willing and able to complete the purchase.*

❖ *To keep your deal moving forward toward completion, any offer should include deadlines imposed on the seller (to respond to the offer) and the buyer (to conduct due diligence, obtain needed funds and get other approvals necessary) so escrow can be closed. Typically, buyers and sellers are granted seven to ten business days to conduct their due diligence work.*

❖ *Finally, the offer should provide a summary of what things need to take place, such as opening escrow and following escrow instructions, in order to complete the transaction.*

❖ *If the subject business is owned by a corporation, the offer and the resulting agreement should declare whether the subject of the sale is the assets of the corporation or the corporate stock. A useful analogy is the toy box: the assets are the toys; the corporate entity is the box containing the toys. The vast majority (some 90%) of small business transfers in California involve the sale of assets. Stock transfers occur in only one in ten business sales.*

❖ *Buyers usually don't want to buy the corporation because of the liabilities they might inherit. There are occasions, however, when taking over the corporation is the only way to maintain certain valuable agreements that belong to the corporation and may not be transferable.*

CHAPTER TWELVE

NEGOTIATIONS

Here's the problem.

As the seller of a small California business, you'd like to get the highest price you can, as quickly as possible. There's nothing wrong with that. In fact this objective is consistent with your method of running your company. You typically work to get the maximum return on your efforts and you frequently operate with a sense of urgency – the sooner, the better.

However, the likely buyers for your business, even those who are most interested in what you have to offer, have the opposite goal – at least when it comes to purchase price and terms. They want to give up the least amount of money possible to get your company, and they want the easiest, most flexible terms – even to the extent that some may ask, in an offer, that you substantially reduce your price and then provide them low interest financing for nearly the entire amount.

And you may yell and scream when you see the offer. But you can't blame them.

With these differences in objectives at play, you may worry that you won't be able to come to a meeting of the minds with a qualified buyer over the sale of your business. In fact, if someone was to agree to your price and terms it might worry you. Maybe he or she is too compliant – not tough enough to make it in your business. Or, you worry that maybe you should have asked for more. If someone agrees to pay the price you requested, does it mean you could have gotten a better price by starting higher?

Welcome to the challenging discipline of negotiations, where it's often necessary to do the "very difficult," and sometimes you have to achieve the "impossible." And just to make things more interesting, you're attempting to do the deal yourself, without benefit of an intermediary to bring the much needed outsider's view and the objectivity that can sometimes facilitate agreement between two parties with opposing agendas.

If you're to have any success at all when you and a buyer arrive at a mutual interest in having a deal, but disagreement about how to get there, it might help to review some of the basic principles of negotiating.

It's Not Personal

You should know, for instance, that there's little room for emotions when talking about your money. For some people, of course, the fear of loss or the anticipation of gain can evoke strong feelings, and these get revealed in a display of one kind or another. But it's best if you can control the outward signs of your anger, elation, sadness, frustration or whatever you are feeling when your proposals are rejected, or even when your suggestions are adopted, as you conduct discussions with a potential buyer.

The necessity of separating emotions from business should seem obvious. And yet I have seen intelligent, successful business owners who react as if they or their company is being criticized severely, when a buyer explains the reasons for not wanting to meet the seller's asking price.

Can you separate your business dealings from the emotional investment you've made in your company? Your outbursts may aggravate, scare, intimidate or even please the people sitting on the other side of the table. But it's unlikely the buyer prospects will change their minds about something because of your behavior. And if you are able to keep your feelings in check, you'll come across as a more powerful figure – someone to be reckoned with – and that can help you get some of the concessions you want.

If so, you'll be able to manage your side of the negotiations from strength, rather than feel vulnerable, victimized and a little scared.

Don't Take Your Eye Off the Ball

When you're in the middle of a battle about a particular subject, just don't lose sight of what you're trying to accomplish. With a clear objective that you keep in your head – a vision of a completed deal to work for – you're less likely to find yourself heavily engaged in a battle over matters that are much less consequential than your goal. Don't allow yourself to be distracted. And don't fix on a particular issue that's relatively unimportant to you, compared to the accomplishment of the overall objective.

That means, for example that you'll recognize the value of a "bird in hand."

Indeed, a prospective buyer may be quite difficult to deal with. And you may feel yourself being pushed toward your limits of patience as well as to the edge of your willingness to negotiate. But are you sure you'd be better off starting from scratch? What if it takes awhile to get another offer? What if the next buyer isn't any better than this one?

Consider this: You've put the company on the market – taken on the hard work, endured the difficult circumstances and maintained patience during the long process – so that you can find a new owner and get fair compensation for your small California business. Let that be your mantra when you encounter issues that threaten to derail negotiations with someone who might be the right buyer, prepared to offer a fair deal for your company.

I'm familiar with a situation in which the seller of a Northern California plumbing supply business was determined to save taxes by allocating the purchase price of his business into capital gains types of assets. He rejected a nearly full-price offer that asked for some of the proceeds to be assigned to the covenant not to compete, which would be taxed at the higher, ordinary income rate.

It was not until months later, after a fall and winter of showings but no offers, that he finally got another proposal. It was structured the way the seller wanted, but at a substantially reduced price, compared to what he asked. In accepting this deal, the seller regretted not moving on the earlier offer. Yes, the original deal would have required him to fork over an additional $14,000 in taxes upon the sale. But considering the lower price in the accepted offer, this seller would have come out ahead had he gone with the proposal made six months before.

Not only is it useful to give extra weight to the 'bird in hand" when considering whether to invest the time and energy involved in trying to make an offer work, it also is beneficial to remember the importance of getting a "bird that can fly." I'm truly surprised at the number of intelligent, business oriented sellers who are so pleased at the idea of getting their price and terms, or close to them, that they don't seriously question the ability of the buyer to succeed in the business. Somehow they forget that if the buyer isn't successful in the business, the seller will have difficulty getting all the money agreed to in the deal.

It is in your interests that the business continue successfully under its new ownership, that the payments you expect will, in fact, be made on time, that you don't have to face a lawsuit if the buyer is failing and blaming you for the problem, that your reputation in the community is not jeopardized by the complaints and criticism of a buyer if he or she is unable to make the business pay off.

Remain Flexible

Another behavioral quirk of people selling their small California businesses is the tendency to become adamant about certain provisions in a transaction without evaluating the overall impact of these issues on the deal. The story, just noted, about the plumbing supply business seller is an example of what can happen when you get fixated on one component of an agreement – in that case it was the allocation of purchase price – and let it ruin an otherwise good transaction.

Certainly, there are matters about which you need to be firm. Some parts of your offering are critical to the overall deal, and it might not make sense to enter into a transaction if your most important needs are neglected. But be selective about what provisions are true deal killers and which are not.

By focusing on your main objectives, you may be able to consider requests for you to agree to a longer pay off period than you'd wanted, or to accept a lower interest rate than you requested, or even to get a new premises lease. These need not be deal killers if there's a way you can accommodate the buyer and keep the transaction on track.

Most every business broker can cite examples of sellers who became stubborn, rather unnecessarily, over relatively minor matters, and then realized, later on, that they might have had a good deal, had they practiced a little flexibility. The business owner who plans to sell is well-advised to learn from the regretful thinking of experienced sellers.

Flexibility is crucial if you are to successfully sell your business.

And Consider All the Costs

When a Los Angeles-based employment agency was sold a few years ago, the seller was required, under the training agreement, to stay with the buyer for six months. Initially, that part of the proposal was totally unacceptable to the seller. She'd started the business nearly 20 years before and had worked hard in it. Her reason for selling was to take life a little easier, and there was no way she wanted to be –in her words – "stuck there for another half year." The broker asked her to consider all of the costs involved in her decision. There was the time cost of the business remaining on the market. "Even if the next buyer wants only three months of training, what if it takes another three of four months to find that next buyer?" the broker pointed out.

And he explored the possible cost of selling to this buyer with a shorter training period – provided the buyer would agree. "If the buyer doesn't have sufficient time to learn the business and can't make it work," the broker reasoned, "you run the risk that she'll stop sending your payments. And there's always the risk of a lawsuit if the buyer is unsuccessful. What would all this cost be?" The broker asked.

After carefully reviewing the possible costs involved in not accepting the offer, or renegotiating for a shorter training time, the seller finally decided to go with the proposal in the form it was presented.

The lesson here is that it's best if you consider all of the costs and the risks involved in your decision as to whether or not to accept an offer, and how to respond. Your initial reaction, upon seeing a less than perfect deal, should not dictate your formal response. A fully informed decision includes some thought as to what can happen in the future, and how that can be shaped by the choice you make today.

These useful ideas for coming to the bargaining table with all your wits about you, in what can be an emotional situation, may be helpful as you try to decide what's the best position to take in negotiating for the sale of your business.

You also may be well served with a few tips for keeping negotiations moving forward when they seem stalled.

Knowing Your Threshold

If you know the absolute lowest price to which you'll agree, and the point at which an erosion of the terms you want crosses the line into territory that is unacceptable, you're prepared to use threshold thinking in the negotiations. Assuming that you and a buyer are far apart regarding some of the provisions of the contract for purchase of your business, you can let the other party know that you feel it's worth exploring how a compromise can be reached, and each of you will have to give a little. If you get agreement on this point, it means the other person is willing to try and work out a deal, and will renegotiate where possible.

From there, it's a matter of discussing each of the issues, perhaps moving back and forth among them, trading wins and losses, until either a final agreement is achieved, or it becomes clear that there can't be a deal without moving beyond the bottom line of one or both of you.

For example, if you are unwilling, under any circumstances, to sell below, say $200,000, and the buyer insists that the highest he'll pay is $150,000, it's not worth your time to continue discussing the matter. But if the buyer says "I'd only pay over $200,000 if I had excellent terms," that might be an opening to continue negotiating.

Suppose you comply with the buyer's lenient payoff terms on your carried-back portion of the purchase price, and you also said you'd stay available to train for up to four months (which you don't mind at all, but pretend that it's an awfully big commitment). Now it might be appropriate to inform the buyer that since you have given in the last couple of items, you'd like him to agree to the allocation of purchase price that allows you to achieve your desire to minimize the tax impact.

And if the buyer objects to your down payment request (perhaps it's more money than he's got budgeted and your figure is above his threshold) find out if he can make that figure work, provided he doesn't have to begin sending payments on his note to you for three or four months following close of escrow.

The value of this style of negotiating is that it recognizes each party has a threshold that can't be violated, though you don't reveal your positions. You agree to respect each others' thresholds, to end negotiations if a deal can't be struck within the parameters acceptable to each of you.

But every thing else is fair game, as you work to find some combination of give and take that can lead you to an agreement.

Building from Consensus

Another approach is to explore the issues with the buyer prospect about which you can agree. If you see eye-to-eye about the terms of the deal, the covenant not to compete, and other factors, you can isolate just those few points on which you do not agree. Then you can chip away at those bones of contention, either by meeting somewhere in the middle, or by taking turns granting a concession. Or both.

I've watched skilled negotiators use this technique very effectively. Sometimes when parties to a transaction in progress reach an impasse, someone will say:

"Let's review again the items that we DO agree on. " The object of this exercise, of course, is to concentrate on the positive aspects of your agreement – the areas where you are in concurrence – as a motivation to find a solution for the negotiating points not yet resolved.

Take a Time Out

Experienced negotiators also know the value of postponing further discussion if opposing parties are getting nowhere in their talks. Rather than arriving at the conclusion that there is no way a deal can be struck, why not reconvene in an hour, or in a few days, when tempers have cooled and principals have had a chance to think through their needs and objectives? A buyer and seller may be able to come back after rethinking their positions and work out a satisfactory deal with provisions they couldn't see clearly in the heat of negotiations, before the break.

Of course, the choice to separate temporarily, for a cooling off period, can work to the detriment of an agreement. It's likely, during the time between negotiating sessions, that one or both of the participants will decide they are not willing to continue negotiating with the other person along the same lines

In either event, the choice to "cool it" for awhile, usually gives people the opportunity to gain some perspective on the issues at hand, so each can determine what is in his or her best interests.

If you and the prospective buyer find yourselves spinning your negotiating wheels and not making progress, perhaps a time out is the best choice.

Conclusion

It's easy to get distracted in the middle of negotiations for sale of your small California business, and to believe that the buyer is trying to take advantage of you. But if you try some of the ideas proposed here, you may be able to see the situation in less threatening terms. And that may help you to continue to engage in negotiations until you arrive at a deal that allows you to sell your business along the lines of – if not blissful ecstasy – at least, terms you can live with.

KEY POINTS FROM THIS CHAPTER

❖ *Considering that you, the seller of a small California business, and most any prospective buyer have contradictory objectives, it can be very difficult to negotiate an agreement. And this challenge is compounded in situations in which sellers are their own representatives, not able to benefit from the services of an objective intermediary who can sometimes work out these differences between parties.*

❖ *It's useful to try and keep your emotions in check when talking business. It is understandable that people have strong feelings when their fortunes are at stake in their discussions, but showing anger, frustration, even elation, makes it harder to maintain the "cool head" needed to arrive at intelligent decisions in difficult negotiations. A buyer's desire to pay less than you want for your business need not be interpreted as a criticism of you and the business.*

❖ *By remembering the overall objective – to get the business sold, at fair terms, to someone who will be successful – can help to prevent obsessing about details of a transaction that, in the long run, are not critically important.*

❖ *However, sellers are not urged to agree to provisions that are contrary to their best interests. To decide what is and is not in your best interests, requires that you look at the transaction as a whole and consider long terms costs as well as short term gains.*

❖ *Using the "bird in hand" rule, sellers should look seriously at offers on the table, even if they fall a bit short in the terms desired. There is no guarantee there will be other offers, or that subsequent offers will be improvements on the one under consideration.*

❖ *And sellers are advised, when negotiating, to consider the likelihood of the proposed buyer's success. A deal that is acceptable with a buyer who is able to make the business work, to continue the payments, and to not pose a litigation risk, is preferable to a "better" deal proposed by a buyer who may have problems once taking over the business.*

❖ *When negotiating for the sale of his or her small California business, a seller is advised to count up all of the "costs" not just in money, but also in terms of time and risk, that are likely to be involved by accepting and by rejecting each proposal under consideration.*

❖ *One way to bring parties together on an agreement is for each to determine the "threshold" for every issue – the bottom line regarding price, terms, and the other components of a buy/sell contract. Then try to compromise on terms in a way that the thresholds aren't crossed.*

❖ *Another negotiating strategy to achieve a deal is to start with agreement on every item about which parties are in accord. Then build on this success by trying to reach a fair consensus on the other issues, one by one. Sometimes if there are two problem areas, the resolution is for one party to win on one, the other party gets the second.*

❖ *A time out is an excellent way for people to clear their heads from the intense, stressful experience of negotiating a business deal. Once they've had a chance to gain a broader perspective it may be easier to reach agreement or, alternatively, to see that there is no likelihood of agreement.*

CHAPTER THIRTEEN

THE DEAL

In the preceding chapters, I've endeavored to offer sellers of small California businesses some insight into the tasks of preparing your company to be presented on the market, offering it for sale and – with effective application of some of these principles, not to mention a bit of luck – achieving a satisfactory transaction. The culmination of all your efforts to date, beginning with the decision to sell, is represented by the purchase and sales agreement. This document, which is likely to be the same form used for the offer, articulates the provisions by which you and the buyer are prepared to complete your transaction – the blueprint for your business arrangement. And it is the definitive record, if needed in the future, of the deal by which your business changes hands, putting the buyer in the position of owner, and freeing you to get on with other things in your life.

Armed with this agreement, you're then ready to dive into the due diligence phase of your transaction. Active involvement on your part, even though this process is mostly the responsibility of buyers, may help to make sure things go smoothly, so that your deal can continue to move forward into escrow.

It's valuable for you to know about these milestones: creation and ratification of your agreement and successful accomplishment of the due diligence exercise, so that you know what to expect and are equipped to deal with these vital parts of the process.

What's Included in the Purchase/Sales Contract

As 90% of the purchases of small California businesses involve business assets, rather than corporate stock, we'll confine the discussion to the more common type of transaction.

To see a sample of the purchase/sale agreement you can go to **www.bizben.com/ selling-buying-business-forms.php** and select Conditional Purchase and Sale of Assets Agreement.

Starting with the basics, a purchase/sale agreement on your business will first note the date and identify the purchaser, include name and address of the subject business, then will state the purchase price and detail how it is to be paid. The amount of down payment is noted, then terms of payoff are spelled out, with an exact description of the note structure. For example, if you are carrying back a portion of the purchase price, does the note call for regular monthly payments over a specified time, one or more balloon payments, a delay of payments, or months when payments may be skipped? This is explained in detail in the purchase/sale agreement so the instructions are clear for the escrow holder, who will be charged with the responsibility of drafting the note, or the notes – if there are more than one.

If additional financing is required to complete the transaction, that should be addressed as the next subject in the contact. And it's important to make clear whether obtaining financing is a requirement for the transaction to be completed – that is, a contingency in the deal. The agreement can even specify the finance terms that are acceptable to the buyer, with respect to length of payoff and interest rate charged, so there is no question as to what will be required to remove this contingency.

The escrow holder also will need specific instructions about collateralizing any notes. Will the business assets provide the security? Have you and the buyer agreed on other collateral, such as buyer's personal or real property, to back up the obligation? Details about this part of the agreement need to be included in the buy/sell contract, in the discussion about the promissory notes.

The lease and capital assets

Determination of the leasehold interest belonging to the business is usually treated as the next item in the agreement. Will the lease be transferred as is? Is there a contingency regarding the buyer being able to obtain the lease at the same terms? Is a new lease required as part of the deal?

What follows in the agreement is the detail of items included in the sale. As this text is concerned with the asset sale, I recommend that the individual items be specifically noted, usually on a separate list. Such list should cover all capital equipment, including vehicles, if there are trucks or cars belonging to the business and part of the sale.

Typically the leasehold improvements are included as assets. They may be given a value in the transaction and are used by the owner of the business, and yet these items ultimately might be written off the business books if they are attached to the real estate and belong to the landlord. Leases ordinarily stipulate whether title to leasehold improvements stays with the owner of the real property or with the tenant who owns the business. These improvements in a restaurant, for example, can include the stoves, ranges, hoods, counters, sinks, dishwasher, built-in refrigeration and other fixtures attached to the real property and used by the restaurant owner. In the interest of avoiding disputes, it's best if the lease clearly designates the ownership of trade fixtures that are considered leasehold improvements. That provision within the lease can be referenced in the buy/sell contract so parties are clear about what is included in the sale.

Inventory

Treatment of inventory – how much is anticipated at cost, at close of escrow, and whether it is to be included as part of the purchase price – is a subject that needs to be addressed in the buy/sell document. If the purchase price includes the inventory of parts, supplies and materials, the actual sale price will be adjusted at the closing, by the variation in value of inventory – when it is counted and computed – from the projected amount.

For example, a sale price fixed at $100,000 that assumes a $20,000 inventory value, may be increased to, say $102,000 if the physical count of inventory reveals a total amount of $22,000 at cost. Conversely, the buyer may get the business for $98,700 if the total dollar amount representing inventory is counted and computed at $18,700. With brokers involved in a transaction, and a commission based on total price, the principals usually are encouraged by their broker representatives to include inventory as part of the deal. Inventory inclusion boosts the business sales price, and hence the commission. A seller, however, should handle the inventory in whatever way he or she deems easier and more appropriate to the circumstances.

The opposite approach, which may save the seller a bit of commission, is to have the purchase price include all assets of the business, except inventory. If inventory is paid for in addition to the business, this fact needs to be made clear in the agreement. It is useful here to specify an estimated figure so the escrow holder has an idea of how much to charge the buyer for inventory once it's counted. Also, don't forget to specify whether the inventory amount is to be added to cash collected from the buyer at close of escrow or added to the promissory note that represents the buyer's obligation to the seller.

Employment agreements

It is likely that as part of the deal, you have agreed with your buyer to be employed with the company for a period of time following the close. In most cases, this does not mean you are added to the payroll, but that you take on the assignment of introducing the buyer to customers, suppliers and other individuals important to the functioning of the company. And you will train your buyer in the operation of the business. The terms of this understanding should be noted, as they will be incorporated into a training agreement, prepared by the escrow and presented to you and the buyer at the close. Depending on what you've worked out with the buyer, the training contract may require you to spend some time at the place of business, or to be available by phone for consultation, or both. Usually, the training period is defined in terms of the number of days or weeks that it extends beyond the close.

The other common form of employment contract is the covenant not to compete, in which you agree that you won't be active as a principal, employee or contractor for any firm engaged in the same business as the one your are selling. This agreement also has a specified period after which it expires, usually coinciding with the length of time provided for paying off the note you hold, say three or five years. Thus, when the buyer is finished paying you on the obligation, you no longer are required to refrain from competing with your former business. There should be a geographic definition for the covenant, setting the number of miles from the subject business in which you are not allowed to compete or work for a competitor. The buyer of your tree trimming service, for example, would not want you to conduct that activity within the area – usually a few square miles – where current customers are located. That is understandable. But there is no reason you should not be permitted to open such a business, even the following week, if you were to move to another part of the state. The time and distance require-ments on the covenant need to be included in the contract you have with the buyer. These terms then will be incorporated into the covenant not to compete which, like the training agreement, will be presented to you and the buyer for approval at close of escrow.

Special provisions

Are there any additional agreements made part of your buy/sell contract to deal with special problems? Suppose, for example, the buyer fears the loss of business if a major customer – rumored to be moving from the area – does relocate soon after close, and the company (when it belongs to the buyer) loses the customer's business. If you agreed to compensate the buyer for part of this loss – provided that move occurs – in order to complete your sale, the exact understanding about this matter needs to be included in the buy/sell agreement. Most likely, the precise terms of this understanding, including the way to determine the compensation and how it is paid (in cash, deducted from note or by some other means) will be reduced to writing in the form of an addendum in escrow. This will be among the papers you and the buyer will sign at close of escrow. And if action taken under this provision will impact the terms of the promissory note, the note should be prepared so as to recognize the special agreement. It might refer to the agreement and include language that explains how the terms of the note are to be altered in the event the provision is enacted.

Items excluded

In many cases, there are items which are present in the place of business that are not included in the deal. It may be sufficient for you and the buyer to agree to a standard provision in your contract which states that anything not on the list of assets transferred is deemed to be excluded from the sale.

But it doesn't hurt to create a separate list of excluded items for inclusion in the contract, so there is no confusion or misunderstanding about what is and is not to go to the buyer at the close.

Some years ago, the buyer of a children's clothing store on the San Francisco Peninsula became upset when he took possession of his business and realized that a number of antique dolls that were prominently displayed when he viewed the business, were no longer at the premises. After a few angry phone conversations, he learned that the seller had taken these items and had not considered them to be part of the deal. An argument followed in which the parties threatened to sue one another over this matter.

The dispute was kept out of court with a final settlement in which some cash went back to the buyer. The parties recognized, after the aggravation they experienced and the payments made to their lawyers to work out a compromise, that they should have compiled a list of items excluded from sale at the beginning of their negotiations.

Understood to be excluded from an asset sale are some items that are found listed on the balance sheet of the business. It's unlikely that you expect the buyer to keep your assets such as the cash on hand. Receivables usually remain with the seller and it is your responsibility to collect them. Even after the close. It's not uncommon, however, if receivables come in – for example to a retail store – for the buyer to collect money owed to the company when conducting the normal course of business, then turn the collections on the receivables over to the seller. Naturally, it's important to keep good records so both parties know who is entitled to which funds.

An alternate plan is for the buyer to purchase the receivables at a discount (commonly between 50% and 80% of their face value), in which event the buyer keeps all money coming in, even those funds paying for business conducted before the transfer of ownership.

Items on the other side of the balance sheet ordinarily stay with the seller as well. Long term debt should be paid off or otherwise handled by the seller so any capital assets taken by the purchaser can be transferred free of encumbrances. Additionally, the payables are deemed to belong to the seller unless there is a specific provision in the agreement to the contrary.

And any special arrangements you've worked out with your buyer regarding long or short term debt should be clearly explained in the contract and will likely be incorporated into addenda, promissory notes, and/or other documents included for approval with the closing papers.

Some deals use the assumption of obligations by the buyer as a way of reducing cash requirements to close escrow. If, for example, the seller owes $30,000 in trade payables, the buyer may decide that by assuming these obligation and paying them off in

90 days, he or she can hold back that amount of cash, using it to promote the business growth, rather than including the funds as part of the down payment. The obligation is then paid out of proceeds from the business. In effect, the buyer arranged for a 90-day loan (usually at low interest). This is likely to be okay with a seller who had planned to use that money to eliminate the $30,000.00 short term debt at the close. Of course, it's necessary to get the approval of the creditors – suppliers and providers of service to the business, who are owed the $30,000. If this strategy is enacted, the contract and the closing instructions must specify that the buyer, in taking over the business, is assuming the $30,000 obligation that was incurred prior to the transfer of ownership.

Perhaps the seller is noticing in this discussion, that there are assets which might be considered part of the deal, but are not. And there are assets and liabilities which ordinarily are not transferred but might be part of an agreement under special provisions. These deviations from standard practice allow parties to customize an agreement for their circumstances.

And whenever changes of this type are made, to reach a mutually beneficial understanding, it's imperative they be written out clearly and thoroughly so the escrow holder knows what documents to prepare for closing, and so that parties to the transaction don't have unnecessary confusion and misunderstandings

Contingencies

After laying out the parts of your agreement, noting what is being sold and for how much, the contract deals with the procedures needed for the transaction to be completed.

Just as the buyer and seller in the transaction for a home use contingencies to protect themselves from having to perform till all the required actions are completed and the facts are in, you and your buyer are waiting for certain things to take place before you move forward. It is the contingencies part of your agreement which outlines the work you both have to do and describes what has to be satisfactorily resolved in order for the transaction to proceed to the next step. We already have touched on a number of these contingencies. They cover the transfer, renewal or rewriting of the lease, the buyer's satisfactory review of the business books and records, the buyer's ability to obtain a certain amount of financing and also the satisfactory inspection and review, by the buyer, of any other issues that pertain to the viability of the business. Whatever they are, all contingencies need to be clearly stated in your agreement so that both buyer and seller know exactly what needs to take place to have a deal, and what might prevent moving forward.

Unlike other components of the transaction, however, the contingencies are not usually included in the escrow papers, for the reason that these items should have been resolved prior to getting into escrow, and are no longer at issue at that point.

As noted earlier, the buyer's time limit to review the business records and remove this contingency should be brief enough to keep things moving forward at a steady pace. While seven to ten business days is a usual time frame for the buyer's conduct of due diligence, there may be delays if you are waiting for the landlord's participation so the buyer can verify that the lease will be satisfactorily transferred or that a new lease, acceptable to the buyer, will be granted. If you're dependent on a lender because of a financing contingency, there also may be a delay past your seven to ten day deadline while the buyer's money sources cross their "T"s, dot their "I"s, and determine if and when the cash will be forthcoming.

Here's your chance to be the hero and keep moving your deal through this step. If you followed the advice offered in an earlier chapter (about preparing your business for sale) you may already have "shopped" the company's borrowing needs and all you have to do is produce a qualified buyer to get the loan started. I also advocate that buyers work on getting pre-approved while searching for a business to buy. This way, buyers can quickly get the money needed, and can demonstrate to skeptical sellers that they're ready and able to do business.

Despite the best planning, of course, there may be delays that are out of your control. That's when it's a good idea to make certain you and your buyer remain in contract. You each can sign a separate note or jointly approve an addendum that refers to the contract and stipulates that you're both in accord about the likely delay and about a new deadline for contingency removal.

And what about your contingency removal? You may need some time – the same seven to ten days is recommended – to verify the buyer's creditworthiness and satisfy yourself that this is a suitable candidate for new owner of your business as well as someone to whom you're willing to loan money.

Escrow

At this point in the agreement, you and the buyer can include the name and address of the escrow holder, and set out a plan for the buyer to deliver, to escrow, his or her deposit check – the one that was presented to you with the offer. It's customary for the buyer to increase the deposit when opening escrow and this provision should be included in your agreement. Also, determine who will pay for escrow services. They start at about $1,000 to $4,000 (depending on size of transaction) for the most basic of escrows, including fees and charges for the preparation of other documents and for the work needed to comply with the law and complete your transaction. Local business brokers can make recommendations as to competent escrow holders and you can find some able escrow services in the resources section at **www.bizben.com** While the question of who pays this cost is sometimes determined with further negotiations between buyer and seller, the parties usually make the choice to split the escrow expenses, and this is recommended as the easiest way to resolve the matter. If you're in the mood to do a little more wheeling and dealing, you can use this point as a bargaining chip. If, during negotiations, the buyer is resisting an idea that's important to you, perhaps you can prevail by offering to pay all escrow fees if the other party will go along with you on that point. Alternatively, when it comes time to insert into your agreement who will pay for the escrow service, you may want to remind the buyer of your last concession during the negotiations, and then announce: "you owe me one," suggesting that the other party pick up the escrow's bill.

The date for closing the deal should be the next entry into your contract. Don't forget the ticking of the clock that will occur while the work is being done to remove contingencies. That should be completed and contingencies removed before escrow is opened. And then there is a roughly two or more week period during which time the escrow is opened, the notice of bulk transfer is published (more about this later), and the 12 business day "window" required by the State of California, is open for any creditors of the business to submit their claims. Keeping these time consuming projects in mind, you can refer to your calendar and decide when you and the buyer can schedule the transfer to take place.

We'll cover the escrow time requirement in a bit more detail in subsequent pages. For now it's important that you realize that even an accepted offer may require a month or so to mature into a closed transaction. This is particularly useful to keep in mind if you're attempting to close a deal before a specific time. More than one seller who failed to allow enough closing time was surprised and disappointed to learn that a deal would drag over into the following fiscal or calendar year, rendering a seller's clever tax planning totally unusable.

The legal provisions

The final paragraphs of your buy/sell agreement will likely include some of the language that lawyers have added over the years, meant to clarify issues and install procedures that can help keep you and other small California business sellers and buyers out of court.

The representations and warranties wording that should go in at this point in the contract, make it clear that the buyer will fully investigate the business and will purchase it only if satisfied as a result of that investigation. The idea here is to protect you from someone who has buyer's remorse and claims to have been somehow forced, coerced or tricked into making the purchase. A common provision, usually added here, is that if the buyer can't or won't put up the rest of the money after removing contingencies, or fails to perform in other respects, the buyer's deposit money, sitting in escrow, will be considered liquidated damages and will be paid to you for your time and trouble.

There also are some protections for the buyer that belong in this section of the contract. They include your representations to the effect that you're not aware of any conditions or circumstances that will negatively impact the business. That means, as we noted earlier, that if you are aware of new competition moving into the area, or some other factor that would impact the business, you should have revealed that to the buyer – preferably in writing, with the buyer's signed acknowledgment that he or she received this information from you.

You'll also be asked to declare that as far as you know the equipment all is in good working order and the inventory is merchantable. That means, there's no reason you're aware of that the inventory would be rejected by customers because it's too old, out-of-date or otherwise unwanted and unsaleable.

Non-disclosure reminder

Because the buyer's careful handling of your confidential information is so important, I recommend repeating the idea that you want your secrets to remain secrets throughout the process in which the buyer is investigating your business. It might be worth adding a paragraph at the end of the agreement with your buyer that reiterates the importance of non-disclosure. In signing the contract for the purchase of the business, the buyer should be reminded about this principle.

Due Diligence

With a signed agreement under your belts, you and the buyer move from the arms-length attitude marking negotiations, to a new level of intimacy in your business dealings. From this point on, it is hoped you'll be working together.

You're hard effort is not over, of course. The buyer may have a number of questions for you, and you should be prepared to provide assistance in any way you can, as the soon-to-be new owner works out the beginnings of a relationship with the landlord, tries to make sense of your financials, looks at your advertising, pours through invoices, customer orders, payroll records and the business check register.

This is not the time to relax. I can recall deals that went bad in the eleventh hour because the seller was not actively engaged in making sure of the buyer's progress during the important process of due diligence. In one situation, a seller took a little celebratory vacation – a bit prematurely it turned out – leaving the buyer alone with the business information at the office of the seller's accountant.

In walked the seller's former partner, a man with whom the seller had experienced a serious falling out years before. This former partner had gone on to become involved in other enterprises, failing at each one, and continuing to carry a grudge against the seller, as well as many other people with whom he'd been involved.

In fact, the former partner did not get along well with others, and besides, was not a trustworthy individual. But the buyer had no way of knowing that. And after the buyer spent the afternoon hearing angry criticism of the seller coming from the former partner, the buyer concluded he wanted to no part of the deal. When the seller returned to town he learned that the buyer had rescinded his agreement to purchase the business

The seller later learned what had occurred and considered suing the former partner for the damage – he'd lost a sale – resulting from the slander. Ultimately the seller concluded it was his own fault for not being present while the buyer was learning about the business.

My advice to sellers is to be involved at every step of the buyer's due diligence, including meetings with landlords, key vendors and anyone else whom the buyer feels should be contacted while the business is under scrutiny. This is certainly what brokers do to make sure a deal is going to work.

If you've reached the point of achieving an accepted offer on your business, you have come too far to cut back on your efforts.

For Franchises

If you operate a franchised business the contract form may be supplied by the franchisor, which also may be able to act as the escrow holder (or may insist on it). Determine if you, or the buyer, or both, will pay for franchise transfer fees, if any. Some franchise owners don't get assistance from the franchisor when it comes to selling. If that includes you, it might be a good idea to include franchisor approval of the transfer as a contingency.

Conclusion

The hard work of preparing a business for sale then marketing it to qualified buyers is starting to pay off when you have identified a buyer with whom you can achieve an acceptable plan by which to sell your small California business.

The buy/sell contract that you and the buyer hammer out after you've engaged in negotiations provides the blue print for that plan. The agreement reviews the details – the price, terms, and allocation – for your transaction. And it lists precisely what is and what is not included in the transaction. The contingencies are noted along with the time in which they are to be removed. An escrow company should be named and you and the buyer will be prepared to take the buyer's check to open an escrow as soon as the due diligence process is completed.

And that, the critical due diligence, needs your utmost attention as the seller of the business. No one else understands and can sell the business, and can reassure a hesitant buyer, the way you can.

KEY POINTS FROM THIS CHAPTER

❖ *Having reached agreement with a buyer on the sale of your small California business, you can now begin your march toward escrow by completion of the buy/sell agreement (often expanding on the document in which the offer was made) and the management of the due diligence process.*

❖ *Some 90% of small California business sales involve the transfer of business assets, as distinct from corporate stock sales. This review focuses on the more common type of transaction.*

❖ *A sample purchase/sale agreement can be viewed and downloaded by visiting **www.bizben.com/selling-buying-business-forms.php** Click on Conditional Purchase and Sale of Assets Agreement.*

❖ *The buy/sell agreement begins by noting the date and identifying the purchaser and the business. That's followed with a description of agreed-on price and terms, including allocation of the price.*

❖ *Seller financing should be explained in detail so that parties are clear about what was agreed, and so that escrow has explicit instructions for preparation of needed documents, such as any promissory notes.*

❖ *Also included is the description about contingencies related to financing and to an acceptable lease.*

❖ *A clear statement of what is included in the sale – a complete list of capital assets is recommended – should be the next part of the buy/sell contract. Another provision is the statement of parties' agreement as to inventory – will a certain amount (at cost) be included in the sale price or considered an addition to the price?*

❖ *Employment contracts in the buy/sell agreement usually refer to the seller's obligation to train the buyer – with specifics about where and for how long that will take place – and to not compete with the buyer's new business for a specified period of time in a defined geographic area. The covenant not to compete is often timed to expire when the buyer's obligation to the seller – if the seller is financing part of the purchase price – is paid in full.*

❖ *Any special arrangements or understandings agreed on by parties should be explained in detail so there is no confusion about this part of the deal, and so that the escrow holder is equipped to prepare any supporting documents necessitated by such agreements.*

❖ *Any items not to be included in the business might be listed and approved by buyer and seller so there is no misunderstanding on this point.*

❖ *While the business receivables, generated prior to the sale, are kept by the seller, it is not uncommon for the buyer to collect them on behalf of the seller, or to buy them at a discount.*

❖ *Sellers expect to pay off the company's short term and long term debt and turn over the business free and clear of obligation. However, if the buyer agrees to assume some of the debt – and that's okay with the creditor – it can help to reduce the amount of cash needed to close escrow. Frequently the buyer can use the money to improve the business.*

❖ *Any contingencies agreed on by the parties, that need to be satisfied and removed prior to opening escrow, should be specified in the buy/sell contract. Contingencies probably include buyer obtaining the premises lease and being satisfied with a review of the business books, records and other information. And you, the seller, may make the deal contingent on being satisfied after your review of the buyer's financial standing and credit worthiness.*

❖ *The agreement then takes up the matter of escrow: Who will conduct the escrow, what the escrow will be required to do and who will pay the escrow fees? A 50/50 split of escrow costs between buyer and seller is a common practice.*

❖ *An anticipated closing date is noted, after parties add in the time that will be needed in order to comply with California's legal requirements for a bulk transfer of business property.*

❖ *Toward the end of the agreement, buyers and sellers add their representations and warranties to provide protection for each other. The buyer acknowledges that he or she will conduct due diligence and rely on those findings to decide whether to go forward with the purchase. The seller warrants that equipment is in good, working order, the inventory is merchantable, and that there are no known factors, undisclosed to the buyer, which might affect the fortunes of the business. Buyers often agree that if they fail to complete the transaction after removal of contingencies, their seller will be allowed to collect the buyer's money on deposit as liquidated damages.*

❖ *The seller might want to repeat the earlier non-disclosure provision in the buy/sell agreement, to remind the buyer about the importance of maintaining confidentiality regarding the transaction.*

❖ *Sellers do well to remain closely involved in the buyer's due diligence work. A number of sales have gone off track at this point and may have been saved had the seller intervened when the buyer ran into questions or problems.*

❖ *There may be delays in the process as buyer and seller are relying on others – lenders and landlord, for example – to be involved in the work of removing contingencies. It is useful for the principles in the transaction to agree in writing to any extensions of the deadlines, necessitated by these delays, in order to remain "in contract."*

❖ *Franchise business owners may find the franchisor has provided all the resources needed to establish a deal and conduct escrow. If not, your contract with the buyer should be contingent on franchisor approval of the sale.*

CHAPTER FOURTEEN

SELLER'S TAX CONSEQUENCES

If you're getting the impression, in your reading of these ideas, that it's always the buyer who encounters unwanted surprises, imagine what can happen when a seller learns after closing a deal on his small California business, that much of the proceeds will be collected by the IRS.

That's a nasty kind of a reality check. And it's a reminder about the importance of planning ahead when selling your company. This reminder was first suggested, some pages back, when the discussion focused on the recommended preparations before your business goes on the market. We observed that it's best to work out an allocation of purchase price beforehand.

The purpose in treating tax consequences in more detail in this chapter is not to give you great tax advice so that you're prepared to beat the system. It's the job of your tax attorney or accountant to recommend the best way to structure your business for sale, based on a number of factors, including your overall financial circumstances, the type of planning in which you've engaged previously, and the relative values of the assets you're selling.

My purpose is simply to urge that you seek out that advice and to let you know how important it might be in determining how much money you get to keep, net of taxes, of the proceeds from the sale of your business. These next few pages will offer an overview of the taxability of your assets, and familiarize you with a few general rules so that you can begin the tax plan part of your sale.

But remember that it is your tax advisor who can verify that you're doing the most intelligent things to reduce the tax bite at the time of your sale. And ask for help fine tuning your plan so you can enjoy maximum benefit from your strategy.

Allocating the Purchase Price

U. S. Tax Law regards the sale of your business as a taxable event and holds you responsible for determining a specific value for each asset sold, enabling the IRS to calculate the amount of any taxes due. The purchase price allocation is the mechanism with which you declare the amount of the total price assigned to every item in the deal. So, for example, when you present your offering to the marketplace, you may declare that the $250,000 asking price includes $80,000 of capital equipment, $100,000 in goodwill, $15,000 for leasehold improvements, $30,000 for inventory (at cost), and the balance of $25,000 divided equally between the training you'll provide for the buyer and the covenant not to compete.

Where exactly do these numbers come from?

The amount allocated to inventory is likely to be the closest to actual cost of all your assets. If a physical inventory at close of escrow reveals that in fact, you have $30,000 invested at cost in this asset, there is no taxable event. You enjoyed no gain; suffered no loss.

That leaves the remainder of assets possibly subject to taxation. And because each item will fall into either one or the other of two broad categories of taxable assets, your allocation should be designed to distribute them in a way that minimizes tax exposure.

The two tax classes, as you probably know, are ordinary income – assessed at your tax rate based on earnings, and capital gains tax – prescribed by laws covering capital assets. As ordinary income is usually taxed at a higher rate than capital gains, you probably want to allocate as much of the proceeds from your sale into this category. That's the guideline followed in the allocation noted above.

Ordinary Income Items

The revenue received as a consequence of most every employment agreement is considered to be ordinary income, taxable at the higher rate. Your promise to train a buyer for three months following close of escrow is an employment contract, even though you haven't been added to the payroll. Also considered an employment agreement is your covenant not to compete. In this case you are agreeing not to work, and the payment you receive under this contract is regarded as nothing but ordinary income, similar to wages, commissions or consulting fees.

Any wonder why, in the example above, the total portion of the purchase price allocated to the items subject to ordinary gain is only 10% of the total? And everything else on the list of assets is considered a capital asset, subject to a lighter tax hit, and so is granted a much higher figure in the allocation.

The simple plan here, of course, is to report the lowest possible value for assets taxed at the higher rate, and a higher value for those items subject to less taxation. But there's an added challenge for all parties involved in the sale of a small California business: Any allocation favoring the seller's situation is probably detrimental to the buyer's tax plan. And visa versa.

This means that even when an agreement about price, terms, length of training and covenant is achieved, you and the buyer may have to return to the negotiating table to work out an allocation to which both sides can agree. And I do recommend that you each report the same allocation. Some buyers and sellers feel they should be entitled to apply their individual valuations to the assets that change hands. In other words, they agree to not agree on this matter.

It's a risky tactic however, because if the IRS happens to choose their transaction as one of the deals it picks out at random for a compliance review, it likely will disallow both allocations, on the basis that they don't agree. This agency of the Federal Government reasons that if a seller received a certain sum for an asset, such as a company's goodwill, that figure should be the exact amount paid by the buyer. Finding a discrepancy, the IRS will probably rewrite the allocations in a way that requires parties to pay the maximum amount of tax.

Capital Gains

Calculations of tax exposure for capital assets is more complicated, compared to ordinary income, because it's necessary, first, to determine the book values of the assets, and then to compare those sums to the values declared in the allocation. Any gain (where allocated value exceeds book value) may subject you to a capital gains tax, and a decline may mean a loss that you can use to balance out gains taken elsewhere.

As you may be aware, the book value of each asset is arrived at by various computations over the period that your business owns it. Every time an asset, such as a piece of equipment, is acquired, the amount paid for it is entered in the appropriate category on the plus side of your balance sheet. Then depreciation charges logged into your operating statement each year represent the amount to be deducted from that total asset figure for the period. In many businesses with active programs of acquiring and selling assets, there are a number of additions and subtractions applied to the assets column of your balance sheet. This is applicable to equipment and leasehold improvements and some "soft" assets like patents, licensing contracts and, in some industries, customer lists.

Notice that inventory, also called stock in trade, is not subject to this accounting treatment. It is a separate asset, its value fluctuating in response to constant additions to and depletions from stock of inventory. The way to measure the worth of this asset is to count all the inventory items – for example dresses, suits, slacks, socks, shirts and similar goods held for resale in a clothing store – determine the cost of each, and then compute a grand total.

Of all the assets in your business, it is inventory (as noted above), which has a book value closely matching its current cost. There is less connection between book and market value in the case of other assets, however, because once entered onto your books, the numbers representing asset value are subject only to accounting procedures. Meanwhile, the items themselves will go up or down in market value based on the familiar rules of supply and demand, without regard to what your balance sheet says.

This means that if you sell a 10-year-old tire changer used in your auto repair shop, it may bring a figure (perhaps more than hundred dollars) that is much greater than its book value (depreciated down to zero). When all of your assets are turned over to a buyer in the sale of your small California business, this same dynamic is at work – the sum collected for equipment will most likely exceed, by a substantial sum, what the balance sheet says it is worth. This is recognized as the recapture of your depreciation, or a capital gain.

Among the most difficult of assets to value is the soft asset of goodwill. Many businesses may carry only a token amount assigned to this category on their books. And yet if the company has little left in depreciable hard assets on the balance sheet and sells for a substantial price reflecting its high profitability, there may be little choice but to assign a sizeable portion of the price to the goodwill portion of the purchase.

It's not a favorite for buyers. They want to buy assets that can be written off (depreciated or amortized) quickly, to enjoy some tax savings in the years ahead. The write off rules for the goodwill asset, however, require a very slow depreciation pace, up to 15 years, so buyers can only shelter a small amount of income each year through depreciation of the sum allocated to the goodwill asset in the purchased company.

As if these principles aren't complicated enough, consider the fact that you'll probably receive payments on the seller-financed portion of the sales price over a period of years after the deal closes. That means part of your tax exposure for the business sale will be parceled out over the period that you are collecting on the proceeds. And you may not know what your tax bracket will be in future years, even though you have to do the planning now. This is all the more reason to consult with a tax specialist, ideally, before your company is placed on the market for sale.

Conclusion

How to allocate your assets and what values to place on each can be a most complicated question. Though we've offered a few guidelines here, the ultimate answers need to be obtained from your accountant or tax practitioner. Whether the components of your sale are subject to tax treatment as ordinary income or as a capital item, can make a substantial difference in the final amount of taxes you pay, and proceeds you keep.

KEY POINTS FROM THIS CHAPTER

❖ *Sellers of small California businesses who fail to tax plan the way the offering is presented, are at risk of paying more taxes than necessary on the sale of the assets.*

❖ *It is strongly advised that you discuss the allocation of purchase price in your business offering with your tax attorney, accountant or other tax advisor before the business goes on the market, and certainly before you enter into a sales agreement.*

❖ *Some general tax planning guidelines are offered so you'll have an overall idea of how the allocation is conducted. But these suggestions are not meant to take the place of the advice provided by your tax expert. He or she is familiar with your situation, and will know how to apply these rules so that you are subject to as little tax exposure as possible.*

❖ *You should be aware that an allocation favorable to a business seller tends to work against the tax saving interests of the buyer. And visa versa. So the allocation of purchase price, in which the assets for sale are assigned to various categories with different tax consequences, may need to be negotiated between you and the buyer of your business.*

❖ *Your agreement to work for a buyer, represented by the post-sale training contract and the covenant not to compete, is considered employment with respect to any income received in return for the work. As such, the values established for these agreements in the allocation of purchase price are subject to taxation as ordinary income, similar to earnings through wages or commissions.*

❖ *It is in the seller's interests to minimize the amount of the purchase price allocated to the training agreement and covenant not to compete, because they are taxed at the higher rate.*

❖ *Also subject to taxes, but at a lower rate, are any gains enjoyed by selling assets at a price higher than their value as listed on the business balance sheet (book value). This is commonly what happens in business sales that include an allocation for equipment at say, market value, when the equipment is shown as having a much lower (depreciated) value by the business. The difference between allocated price and depreciated value is the seller's gain, subject to the capital gains tax rate.*

❖ Usually it is only the inventory of stock in trade, valued at cost, which is worth, in real and current dollars, exactly the figure assigned to it in the purchase price allocation. This being the case, there would be no tax consequences from the sale of the inventory to the buyer. The seller has neither gained nor lost in this part of the transaction.

❖ Assigning a value to the goodwill of a profitable business can be problematic. If there is little in the way of hard assets, the seller wants to include most of the purchase price in the category of goodwill. The amount by which this figure exceeds the goodwill value on the business's balance sheet may be substantial. And when collected, it will be subject to capital gains taxes. Buyers aren't happy to allocate a great deal of value to goodwill as it is slow to depreciate.

❖ An additional aspect of your planning – and another reason you must see your tax advisor – concerns the timing of your receipt of the sales proceeds. If you collect all cash at close of escrow, the tax hit is probably going to come in a single year. If you finance for the buyer however, the principal part of your annual income on the note may be apportioned according to the allocation of purchase price. In that case, your planning needs to account, not only for how the allocation has been established, but also what your anticipated earnings from other sources will be during the years you also receive money from the sale of your business.

CHAPTER FIFTEEN

FINANCING

It was suggested, early in this book, that one of the ways to prepare your small California business for sale is to line up some extra funds to help a capable buyer make the purchase at your price and terms. If the buyer is short of meeting what you need, maybe there's a source of cash you can call on to make up the difference. And now that we're deep into the mechanics of your sale – having talked about preparing, marketing, finding buyers and negotiating a deal – it's an appropriate time to give you some ideas about how you would go about raising an extra twenty, fifty or even more thousands of dollars to make your transaction happen.

Seller Financing

The number one source of funding to facilitate the sale of a small California business is, as you may have guessed, seller financing. In roughly 60% of the instances of small business sales in California, some of the money needed to complete the purchase has come from the seller. The standard arrangement is for the buyer to give the seller a cash down payment for whatever amount the parties have agreed on in their negotiations. Typically, a down payment is between one-third and one-half of the purchase price. Then, if the seller is willing to carry the balance, the buyer will issue a promissory note for that amount in favor of the seller. In most cases, the obligation will call for equal monthly payments over an agreed-on period – often three to seven years – to be paid with interest charged on the unpaid balance. Security for this obligation might be the assets of the business only, or a combination of the business and other property owned by the buyer.

I'm a strong advocate of seller financing as I believe it's an important ingredient in the success of a business that has changed hands. And clearly the offering of seller financing when the company is being marketed sends a message to prospective buyers that it must be a solid business with a good future. After all, the seller is willing to lend money on it and he – or she – should know!

In fact, the seller not only is casting a vote of confidence for the business by offering to help finance the deal, but also is demonstrating an intent to stay involved in the fortunes of the business. If someone owes you money on the company you sold, you'll most likely be willing to offer ideas or advice to make sure that company continues to thrive, and can generate the revenues needed for the buyer to pay off the obligation to you.

Seller financing, of course, can take several forms and need not constitute the entire balance of the purchase price, after the down payment. I've been involved in transactions that used seller financing with some adjustments on the usual theme in order to accommodate the circumstances of the purchase. In one variation, the seller may wait three or six months before the payments begin. This gives the buyer an opportunity to get both feet on the ground in the company, take care of any unexpected cash requirements (there always seem to be a few of those), and to put a few dollars into building up the business. Another alternative is for the seller to receive proceeds due on the note in one or more balloon payments, rather than in monthly installments. This plan works well in a situation where a buyer intends to obtain other financing on the business, or to use different means to raise the funds within a year or so of the transfer. In effect, this tactic is calling on the seller to provide a swing loan – some money to tide the buyer over and complete the purchase – until arrangements can be made for more permanent financing. The seller in this example is not actually giving funds to the buyer, but is postponing collection of money owed, earning some interest on it and giving the buyer time to get the funds needed to retire or pay down the debt to the seller.

I've also seen seller financing structured with more than one note issued by a buyer in favor of the seller. This strategy combines standard seller financing—using a note paid in monthly installments over an agree-on period – with a note due to be retired in six or 12 months. And in one case I know about, in which the seller took a note from a buyer who planned to build up the business for resale, the parties agreed the note would be paid off with accrued interest upon the next sale of the business, whenever that might be.

Along with help financing purchase of the business, the seller often provides other benefits to the buyer, including the offer of advice if needed (hoping to insure that the business will survive and the note will be paid), and flexibility about terms of the deal. It is customary for a business buyer to save one to three percentage points of interest on a promissory note originated for seller financing, compared to a conventional business loan.

While some consultants advise sellers to get every scrap of collateral available when carrying back financing for the buyer, others feel that asking for security beyond the business itself is likely to discourage a buyer from wanting to deal.

My thought is that the way to collateralize such a loan is dependent on a number of factors. If there is a substantial down payment in relation to the size of the obligation to the seller, it probably is unnecessary to collateralize the buyer's note on the remaining sum – besides assets of the business. That's certainly the case if there is enough value in the business assets – equipment, receivables and inventory – to support the amount due.

A highly leveraged deal, however, is a blueprint for disaster if the buyer can't make the business successful enough to support the debt load. If your deal is shaping up in a way that leaves you feeling vulnerable to loss in the event the business goes under, then don't agree to the proposal unless and until the obligation is backed up with the pledge of other security, such as real estate.

And you can be flexible in this area as well. Parts of the collateral can be released over the period of an obligation as it becomes "seasoned." In one case, a five year note was initially secured by the business as well as the buyer's real property. After 18 months of prompt payments on the obligation, it was rewritten to require only the business assets as collateral. I believe this arrangement was needlessly complicated, but it made a deal possible for parties who were split on the issue of using the real estate security for the note. This was the compromise both could accept.

If you, as a seller, are willing to help finance the purchase of your business, and to be flexible in how that is done, you will increase the chances of finding a buyer willing and able to meet your terms.

The Cheapest Conventional Money

While seller financing is likely the best deal a buyer can get on funds needed to complete a purchase, the least costly loan from a conventional source is usually the home equity line offered by many banks and savings and loan institutions.

There's nothing you as a seller can do to facilitate your buyer getting this kind of a loan, because it's not related to the company – your business pre-approval work would not be relevant. But you may want to recommend this approach if your buyer hasn't thought about it and has real property equity. I particularly like the idea of borrowing on home equity, not only because the rates beat business loans, but also because the real estate lending route involves less red tape, requires less reporting and usually gets approved and funded more quickly than most other kinds of business loans. If a buyer has real estate with a value exceeding its mortgages, and a fairly good credit record, there are dozens of financial institutions ready to provide the cash for whatever purpose the borrower wishes to put it.

Many buyers reject this idea because they think simply that they ought to get a business loan to accomplish business purposes. In the case of most loans to purchase a business, however, the borrower is required to put up real property equity as collateral. That's right: When a business bank is called on to lend capital that will go into the down payment on a small company, the borrower is probably going to be asked to put up a second trust deed in the family home or other solid assets, so the lender is protected in the event the business is unable to provide the money needed to service the loan.

It doesn't take a shrewd business mind to figure out that if your real estate equity needs to be pledged anyway, you might as well get regular home equity money with the lower rates and all the other borrower benefits that come with it.

Traditional Sources

Among the most common institutional sources of money for a business acquisition is represented by the network of lenders backed by the SBA (U.S. Small Business Administration). The federal agency will guarantee loans made to purchasers and existing owners of enterprises that comply with its small business definition (up to 500 employees for most companies in manufacturing, a maximum of 100 employees in wholesale trades, a lid on annual revenues – averaged over a three-year period – of $6 million for most firms in retail and service industries, $28.5 million for the majority of businesses involved in general and heavy construction, and $12 million for special trade contractors). A benefit of this program is that borrowers without real estate for collateral still can meet the government agency's qualifications. And with this approval, many institutions will ratify loan requests up to $250,000. But if there are real estate or other available assets in the borrower's portfolio, besides the business, the lenders usually insist on using such assets – up to the value of the loan – as additional security.

What the SBA looks at are four key factors, and at least three of the four should be present for your buyer to qualify with a lender who'll seek the SBA guarantee, and therefore will be more likely to work with you and your buyer than a conventional bank. The factors are: 1. Cash flow of the business; 2. Borrower's work experience as it relates to the business; 3. Borrower's credit history; and 4. Collateral of the borrower, in addition to the business assets, that can be used to secure the obligation.

In the event you find a buyer who has what it takes to satisfy the SBA, you may be able to build some financing for both a down payment and working capital right into the offering of your business by taking advantage of this program. Check out the Resources Section at **www.bizben.com** for an SBA lender contact from whom you can learn more.

You can assemble part of the SBA package – the portion that requires a narrative and financial history of your business – for use in the event you find a suitable buyer who may want this kind of loan for some of the purchase money. The buyer's contribution to the application for an SBA guaranteed loan will be to include his or her work history and a business plan.

Money also is available from some business lenders who will take the company's liquid assets as collateral. It's common for owners of established retail firms to use inventory financing. The money helps them stock up for the holiday selling season, for example. And the inventory either is pledged to the lender to make sure the loan will be retired, or is signed over to the lender, and then released in increments back to the borrower, in return for progress payments.

Receivables financing is another way of using liquid assets to raise capital. Owners of many distribution and manufacturing businesses find that although the company is enjoying good revenues with satisfactory profit margins, most of the earnings are tied up in receivables. Until customers pay their bills, the business might be strapped for the cash needed to expand production, modernize facilities or market more aggressively. One way to improve cash flow in this situation is to pledge the receivables to a business lender for a loan of up to 80% of the value of those receivables. As the company collects the funds owed to it, the loan balance is paid down. And some firms are able to pass along to their slow-paying customers, their cost of borrowing in the form of a one or two percentage point financing charge.

A variation on this idea is for the company to sell its receivables to a factor – someone who'll pay, somewhere between 60% and 80% of the face receivables value, and then will be responsible for getting customers to pay up.

These are fairly common practices used by established businesses with existing lender relationships to ease occasional cash crunches. But there's no reason you can't ask your bank to put up some of the money that will be used for the purchase of your company, and to accept the company's liquid assets for collateral. Inventory or receivables loans may not generate as much cash as a typical SBA-backed lending deal. But for part of a purchase price or for working capital, this may be an ideal source.

And here's another opportunity for you to do some valuable preparatory work before you start marketing the business: Tell your current bank that your company will probably continue to be a customer, under its new ownership, if the bank can help make the deal with a loan secured by the business' liquid assets.

Innovative Financing Strategies

If you've learned anything as owner of a small California business, it is how to solve problems with resourceful planning and creative thinking. You may get the chance to exercise some of these talents if the buyer for your business who needs a little more cash to meet your terms, is unable to get it from traditional sources. Perhaps you like the person's chances of being successful as new owner of your company, but he or she is a little short of having all the cash needed to make the deal work. It might be easier to find the needed money than to find another buyer with more cash. And here are a few places to look.

Just because your bank isn't willing to come up with the $10,000 or $30,000 or whatever you'll need to make the deal, doesn't mean you can't get a "yes" to this proposal by going elsewhere. Other banks, eager for new business, are one alternate source. And check out **www.bizbuyfinancing.com**, a resource which may be able to help your buyer find the extra cash needed to close the deal. Another source is your vendors – the companies supplying your business with the products, materials and services that enable it to function. If they would like to keep doing business with your company, once the new person takes over, perhaps they'll be willing to stretch out the period during which they usually require their bills to be paid.

Ask the grocery wholesaler providing much of the inventory for your corner market if they can wait 45, instead of 15 days to get paid for package and dairy goods. That concession will give the new owner of the business a little extra money for working capital needs, so he or she can dig deeper into current cash reserves and give you the down payment you want.

A variation on this plan – and this idea was expressed in an earlier chapter – is for one or more of your vendors to let your buyer pay your old bills. If your photo lab, for example, owes $25,000 to an outfit to which you send some of the high resolution scanning and digitizing work, can the buyer take on this responsibility in your place? And can the terms of payment be extended? If so, that's another $25,000 not needed immediately for operations, so it can be used to make the deal and close the escrow.

A completely different approach is to acquaint your buyer with a provision of tax law that allows the rollover of IRA or 401K funds into a trust, and permitting funds in the trust to be used for purchase of a business without liability for deferred taxes. In other words, if the buyer has tax protected retirement money in mutual funds or other investments, he or she may think that the deferred tax bill will have to be paid if the money is used for a less passive investment. Not so. A provision of the U.S. Tax Code recognizes the rollover of invested funds into a business opportunity as a transaction that does not interfere with the deferred status of the taxpayer's money. This is a strategy that may make it possible for your buyer to "find" several thousand more dollars to put into the purchase.

If none of these strategies will get you the down payment you need, how about putting the amount of the shortfall into a promissory note, which you can then discount and sell in a few months to get your cash? For sake of discussion, let's assume that the buyer can provide $150,000 of the $200,000 down payment you want. Where will the other $50,000 come from? The strategy suggested here, is that you receive that money in the form of the note and then, after the note has had a chance to "season" – with all payments made promptly for six or nine months – you would ask a note "buy-back" company to take over as the creditor and give you the going rate – probably 80%

($40,000) for the "paper." This enables you to get most of the down payment you want; you'll just have to wait awhile to collect the part that wasn't available when you closed the deal.

One of the nice aspects of this plan is that you don't have to wait till months after your deal closes, to find out if this can work, hoping the whole time that you'll be able to find someone to buy back the note. This is one of the areas in which you can do some planning, as you prepare your business for sale.

By contacting organizations which buy back promissory notes of this type, you can work toward an understanding about what size note can be sold and at what discount rate. Additionally, you can prepare the business-assets side of this understanding. Provide the buy-back organization with the information needed so the business can be pre-approved for the note purchase. At the same time, you can find out what qualifications will be required of a buyer – the person who will make payments to the note holder once you've sold it. Some of the most active note buy-back services can be found by checking out the resources section at **www.bizben.com**

If all else fails, there's one other source of capital which – though I consider it to be the "bank of last resort" – is commonly used by small business buyers and owners to raise money, fast. It involves a plea to the friendly lenders who fill our mail boxes with Visa and Master Card offers. Keep this in mind when your buyer tells you there is no other place to get that last $10,000 or $20,000 needed to close the deal. Most likely there is.

Credit card borrowing comes at a high interest rate to be sure, but if the sum standing between the buyer and your business can be accessed easily with the plastic in the buyer's wallet – and he or she is motivated to take over your company – it's a strategy well worth considering.

After reviewing these suggestions about ways for your buyer to incur additional debt to come up with all the cash you want, you may be reminded of the candidates for political office who pledge to expand services while cutting taxes. The question to ask is: If the buyer is going to incur all these obligations, where will the money come from to pay them?

As owner of the business, you're the best person to address that issue. And before encouraging the buyer to get stretched too thin, it's best that you carefully consider just how much debt you think the business will be able to reasonably support. Remember that the buyer probably won't make as much money as you do, considering the deposits and start-up expenses that will pop up in the early months of the new ownership. And then there is the cost of the mistakes the new owner will likely make while learning the business.

I don't think it's in your best interests to let the buyer get in over his or her head in debt upon taking over. Even if you got your cash at the close, you want the business to continue on, successfully as before. We'll talk about the reasons for this in one of the final chapters.

And you certainly don't want to encourage a buyer with few assets and little cash to pull off a highly leveraged deal on your company. It may be fun to read about how people have taken over organizations with just a hope and a prayer. Stories like this fuel the American dream that anyone can become wealthy if they are sufficiently clever and tenacious.

But not with your business.

Whether your company is highly successful or barely getting by, the odds are against a leverage artist succeeding at buying and building it up. In many cases the over leveraged deals result in the company collapsing under the weight of its own debt. A buyer for your business with little at stake besides some time spent wheeling and dealing, hasn't much to lose if the company can't continue to be healthy. Most likely the biggest loser in a situation like this will be you.

Shared Equity

Rather than dwell on the notion that the buyer is someone you should fear and distrust, let's explore the strategy that sellers can employ to achieve a deal with a buyer who hasn't enough cash to take over the entire company, but is qualified in every other respect – and has your complete confidence.

You can form a partnership or a corporation in which the buyer takes over some or most of the ownership, and does most of the work, with you retaining an interest. Over time, that interest can be bought out entirely.

There are any number of ways to structure such a deal, and plenty of attorneys, bankers, insurance agents (who will arrange to underwrite a buy/sell agreement triggered by the death or illness of you or the buyer), and other consultants who can help you make this happen. That's really the easy part.

The critical question is whether there is enough trust and communication between you and your buyer to make this work.

This strategy is not, of course, as easy and quick as an outright sale. But if there is a solid connection with your buyer and the desire to transfer the business to him or to her, you should explore the idea of "sharing" the company.

Conclusion

Preparation of a small California business for sale cannot be complete unless the seller has explored some of the ways to source additional capital that may be needed to close a deal. Ideally, you'll find a buyer who meets all the requirements and has enough cash on hand to meet your terms. Besides, I encourage sellers to be the bank, to the extent possible, so you, as well as the buyer, have a stake in the business' continuing success. But this isn't an ideal world. So you're well advised to do some back-up planning by determining where the buyer can go for that extra $10,000 or $25,000 or $50,000. And you frequently can get the business pre-approved so that when the time comes to raise the funds, some of the work is behind you, and the process can proceed quickly.

Among the suggestions offered are the traditional resources for business capital including SBA secured money, cash advanced on liquid assets of the business and – perhaps surprisingly – a simple home equity loan. Less traditional techniques include tapping vendors for extensions on the time needed for your business to discharge its accounts payables, and rolling over retirement accounts into tax-protected trusts that can help fund a business. Another strategy for getting your money involves arranging a pre-approval on the business, which will later help sell a somewhat "seasoned" note from a buyer to a buy back service. You also can send the buyer into the eager arms of the banks that want to offer cash and lines of credit accessed through their Visa and MasterCard accounts. Also discussed is the approach that uses equity in the company rather that debt to accommodate a buyer whom you like.

KEY POINTS FROM THIS CHAPTER

❖ *The number one source of funding to facilitate the sale of a small California business – accounting for about 60% of the deals – is seller financing of at least some of the money needed.*

❖ *Seller financing offers a number of advantages in the way it adds to the appeal of the business. And it usually provides affordable purchase money for the buyer.*

❖ *The question of whether to collateralize the note to the seller with business assets only, or with other property of the buyer, is often a point for negotiation when seller financing is involved. There is no single right solution for this matter and sellers are advised to eliminate their risks as much as possible, without putting an excessive burden on the buyer.*

❖ *The cheapest conventional way to borrow is usually with a home equity loan – a preferable deal to most loan packages granted to buy a business. The later come with higher interest rates and more qualifying and reporting requirements, along with the need to put up real estate as additional collateral.*

❖ *One approach to getting an institutional loan for a business purchase, without real estate security, is the program offered by the Federal Government through the SBA. It guarantees business loans from select institutions to those who qualify. Sellers can learn how to help qualify their business for SBA-backed funding by going to the Resources Section at* ***www.bizben.com***

❖ *Lenders who provide receivables or inventory financing might be resources for some of the cash needed to complete the sale of a small California business.*

❖ *Another way to raise money for the seller's down payment is to pre-qualify the business with a service that buys back promissory notes. The seller can discount and sell a note received from the buyer after six or nine months of "seasoning." Some of these services also are found in the Resources Section at* ***www.bizben.com***

❖ *A funding resource especially for small business transactions in California is found on the Internet at* ***www.bizbuyfinancing.com***

❖ *Vendors to the business can be a source of financing if they will agree to let the buyer take responsibility for the seller's payables. This strategy frees up cash to increase the down payment or working capital. Vendors also can cooperate with the new buyer by permitting an extension in payment of their obligations.*

❖ *Sellers might like to know a buyer can roll over his or her retirement account into a trust that can be used to buy a business without triggering any tax consequences*

❖ *The "bank of last resort," using credit cards, is sometimes the solution for a buyer who needs more cash to complete a deal and has no other resources.*

❖ *Sellers often can help their buyers find more money but should be aware of the dangers of overburdening a business with financial obligations.*

❖ *If a buyer can't raise enough money through increased debt to buy all of a business, one solution is to buy part or most of the business and become partners or a corporate shareholder with the seller.*

CHAPTER SIXTEEN

THE WORKINGS OF ESCROW

If you remember the scenes from movies taking place in the Old West, you might recall that when two gamblers had a bet going they engaged a stakeholder to hang onto the cash that each put up and then pass the whole kitty over to the one who drew the most aces, or fired the most silver dollars out of the air with his six gun, or whatever the bet. Or the middleman in a horse sale took responsibility for making sure that the seller showed up with the designated stallion and that the buyer brought all the money agreed on.

The job of stakeholder pretty much describes one of the key assignments of escrow companies hired to handle the documents and the money involved in the transfer of small California businesses in the 21st Century. But things have become a bit more complex since then, so the escrow holder has much more to do than just stuff the cash in one blue jeans' pocket and the business ownership certificate in the other.

And to make sure everyone knows what they're supposed to be doing, California legislators put together a fairly extensive set of rules for such business transactions – rules found in the State's Uniform Commercial code, mostly in Provisions 6102 through 6108.

You'll be glad to know that once you're dealing with the escrow company, much of your work is finally behind you. Ideally you don't open an escrow until contingencies have been removed. That means your buyer is satisfied with everything reviewed during the due diligence examination, the landlord has agreed to cooperate with transfer of the lease or to establish new terms acceptable to your buyer, the franchisor has "blessed" your deal (if your company is a franchise), and any lenders – whether a bank or one of the company's vendors – have approved your requests for their money and cooperation.

You're not finished yet and there could be surprises in the form of unexpected claims coming into escrow. But the clock is starting to tick down to the day when you'll turn over the business, take your money and promissory note and proceed to your next adventure.

Opening Escrow

The first thing you and the buyer will do when opening escrow is to instruct the company about the terms of your deal. As noted earlier, the fee will vary from $1,000 to $10,000 for the basic services. The rate depends on the dollar value of the deal and usually includes the work needed to prepare extra documents and to take care of the filings. Ordinarily the fees are split 50/50 between you and the buyer and the escrow firm will probably want some of the money at the beginning. You also will be asked to sign some documents to get things started.

And here are some of the things that the escrow needs to start:

Lien search

A check of the public records is made to determine the rightful owner of your equipment and fixtures, and if there are any claims on them. Similar to a title search conducted on real property, this procedure is meant to find out if there are any liens on the personal property used in the business. The search is managed by accessing records for property under the name of the business, or its address or both. It's not unusual to discover that the owner before you, or some taxing authority has neglected to remove a lien or claim that has long since been satisfied. And part of the escrow company's job will be to track down the parties and paperwork to verify that the items you are selling to the buyer are free and clear, just as you stated.

Receiving claims

Nothing gets paid out of escrow without your approval, of course, and anyone entering a claim will be required to demonstrate that you indeed owe them money or property before their claim can be honored. You can expect the escrow to hear from government taxing authorities which enter claims as a matter of course, just to make sure no one is able to close a deal without being current with their obligations.

The escrow officer will review and pass along to you any claims that come in and will discuss with you how they are to be handled. In most cases the escrow will speak to you privately about any claims that have come in. In theory, they are not the concern of the buyer unless he or she will be asked to assume a debt or take property subject to an encumbrance. In practice, however, you probably don't want to have any secrets from the buyer – following the "nothing to hide" principle – so you might want to make sure that if any unexpected claims show up, the buyer has your full explanation and reassurance that it is invalid or will be handled.

That means you can go ahead and talk about say, the judgment obtained years ago by an unhappy customer, or other little blemishes in your company's otherwise perfect history.

Notice of bulk sale and ABC License transfer

The public notice of bulk transfer is conducted for the protection of the buyer (so there will be no claims against the business unknown to the buyer – none of those unpleasant surprises), and also for your protection (demonstrating that you complied with California law and can't be prosecuted by the government or sued by a private party for claims coming out of an improper or illegal transfer). This notice will be published in a local newspaper that carries legal advertising with you and/or the buyer paying another $50 or so for this service. As noted in the prior chapter, you can expect at least 12 business days of wait time between the date the notice first appears and the day you can close escrow. This is designed to give any creditors time to notify the escrow - which is named in the notice – that the business owes them money for one reason or another.

And if your business holds a liquor license – either just to sell beer and wine, or approval for full liquor – the escrow will send you and the buyer to your local ABC (Alcohol Beverage Control) office to apply for a transfer. There you will obtain a large (about three feet square) notice that is required to be posted to the window of the establishment. And, like the notice of bulk transfer, make sure to have an announcement about the transfer published in an approved paper. This incidentally, applies to cafes that offer beer and wine as well as to restaurants with a full bar, and, of course, grocery and liquor markets. There also is a waiting period associated with this notice, running concurrently with the wait associated with the bulk transfer. But it takes longer. In many or most cases the ABC Board can spend 60 calendar days or more to complete its investigation of the buyer and the proposed transfer, and in no case does the law permit the license to change hands in fewer than 30 calendar days following posting. And the buyer should make sure to make an application with the planning commission for the town or municipality where the transfer is to take place. They want to make sure the area is approved for the use and that the laws are being upheld.

Requesting releases

Even if no taxing authorities have entered a claim, your escrow holder will request clearances from the State Board of Equalization, the IRS, State Franchise Tax Board and the local employment offices just to make sure that you're up to date in paying sales taxes, payroll taxes, personal property taxes and any other taxes, fees, dues, levies, fines, tolls or added charges your representatives in Sacramento have conjured up lately. It's a good idea to hang onto your cancelled checks and any receipts from these agencies to show you've paid everything due. The government is usually slow to verify the information that you'll need to get clearances, and you may be able to speed things along with the proof of payment in your documentation.

Verifying approvals

A similar procedure to requesting releases is the escrow's job to contact the landlord to confirm the details you provided about the lease transfer. And, with the landlord's okay, the escrow can help in this action by keeping track of the new lease or lease assignment, getting it signed by the parties and delivering copies at close of escrow. If the buyer will be operating under your lease, any prorations needed will be handled between you and the buyer in escrow. If a new lease is involved, with added payments due to the landlord, escrow may include the landlord in this part of the escrow, having him sign relevant documents and issuing a check for any added rental deposit and/or increased rent.

Approvals needed from institutional or non-institutional lenders also can be verified by the escrow holder. And escrow will make sure any necessary funds to be loaned the buyer are ready when needed, and that loan papers have been properly presented and, at the closing, are signed.

Preparing documents

The loan from you to the buyer will need a promissory note to be official, and that is a document which the escrow ordinarily drafts for both, using standard language, and inserting your name, that of the buyer, terms of the loan and a reference to the security agreement, which lists the assets that are used to secure the obligation. Also prepared by escrow can be the other parts of your agreement, such as the covenant not to compete, the training contract and any other deals you and the buyer have made to facilitate the transaction.

Waiting it Out

After these tasks are completed, there may be a lull in activity as you wait for expiration of the mandatory periods associated with the published notices. You might want to focus on making sure the business is running smoothly and the buyer will be busy with preparatory tasks, such as filing a fictitious name statement so he or she is permitted to use your company's trade name. You'll probably be asked to go to the recorder's office in the county where the business is located to sign off on a release of the name.

And there are a couple of other things you can keep in mind as the clock ticks toward the day when the transfer will be complete. One is to maintain the confidentiality about the impending sale and encourage the buyer to do the same. It may be hard to keep the secret at this point; a number of people may have been brought in on the situation, such as the landlord, vendors who are planning to work with the buyer for special finance arrangements, and perhaps an employee or two who were taken into your confidence early in the process and sworn to secrecy in return for the promise of an incentive once the deal closes. But I advocate keeping the information as quiet as possible. In the event something was to go wrong and disrupt your sale, you'd have a lot of explaining to do, not to mention your state of embarrassment.

I realize that it's hard to keep quiet a fact that has become a matter of public record with publishing in the newspaper. Most of your customers and employees probably are not reading the legal notices and you should make every effort not to talk about the sale, even though, technically, it has been made public.

The ABC notice plastered to the front of your window will be hard to ignore. And so you will want to be ready with an explanation for anyone who asks. It's best to tell the truth, but be as succinct about it as possible, sparing others the details of your deal. You still aren't 100% sure it'll happen and you don't want to go into more excruciating facts if the sale, for any reason, can't be completed.

The other project for this period is to confer with the buyer on a training schedule and perhaps plan a little campaign that will go into effect after the close, announcing to customers about the new ownership. This may involve a mailing to everyone on the customer list. Perhaps it will make sense for you and the buyer to pay a call on key clients to let them know the news and introduce the new person. By planning this out now, you'll be ready to implement the program when the time is right.

This is one of those times in the selling process, incidentally, when you will appreciate having done the hard work to prepare your company. The last few items needed by the lender for final okay on the funding to close escrow, are probably at your finger tips by now. The meetings with the landlord and with key vendors will have paid off as they are aware of what's happening, and what must be done so escrow can honor their claims and requirements. Any problems that occurred were probably handled quickly and efficiently with escrow, because you anticipated most everything that might come up at the end, and you planned accordingly.

The Close

On the day scheduled for close, with the wait time fully elapsed and all needed documents and money in place, the escrow will have a few final important steps to follow to make the transfer official.

The buyer will be asked to bring a certified or cashier's check for the closing amount, which will include the balance of down payment, the buyer's share of fees, any deposits to be collected through escrow, any sales or use tax on personal property purchased from you, and the sum of prorated expenses allocated to the buyer.

The rent might be prorated so that you're reimbursed for the part of the month for which you paid rent, but will no longer own the business. You also will probably get your lease deposit back from escrow, an item that is charged to the buyer. Prorations also can apply to rental of equipment, advertising and promotional contracts and other services for which you have prepaid. Personal property taxes also might be prorated.

After documents are signed and checks distributed – the one for you, for the broker if any, for payments to various Federal and State agencies to close your accounts and to any other entity with a legitimate claim, the escrow will file the documents that need to be publicly recorded. Among them is the security agreement listing personal assets that are being pledged to you as collateral for the loan to the buyer. Any other property, including the buyer's real estate – if it is being used to secure the obligation – will be identified in an appropriate filing.

This is when the final inventory count is presented to escrow so you can receive the exact amount of money for this, either as part of, or in addition to the price – depending on the agreement.

Once these tasks are completed, the documents signed and notarized, and question are answered, the escrow holder will send you off to celebrate, so he or she can finish with the paperwork.

Conclusion

This review of the final processes is meant to give sellers an overview of the steps that take place once a transaction for sale of a small California business is moved into escrow. There is not much left for the seller to do except make sure escrow has all the documents needed to comply with the law and respond to any claims from private or governmental organizations if added information is required.

Sellers are cautioned that during the waiting period – 12 business days mandatory for a business not needing an ABC license transfer, and at least 30 days, probably 60 days or more, for a business which serves any form of liquor – it's a good idea to talk as little about the sale if possible. And if there is no public notice plastered to the window of your bar, restaurant or liquor store, you may be able to keep the secret a little while longer.

Once you've closed and received your money, you can announce the achievement to whomever you like.

KEY POINTS FROM THIS CHAPTER

❖ *Much of the California law covering the sale and purchase of small businesses is contained in the Uniform Commercial Code, specifying some of the tasks to be completed before a transaction is closed.*

❖ *An escrow will cost from $1,000 to $10,000 based on transaction size, for the basic services. This should include activities such as drafting notes and filing documents.*

❖ *Among the responsibilities of the escrow are to conduct a lien search, assist with the notice of bulk transfer – and in the case of a liquor license transfer, an ABC notice – receive claims, request releases from taxing authorities, verify approvals from lenders and others whose okay is needed to close, prepare documents such as promissory notes, and confer with the parties about claims in the escrow and prorations of rent and other prepaid expenses.*

❖ *There is a mandatory 12 business-day wait for creditors to present claims following publishing of the bulk transfer notice. Escrow can close on the 13th day.*

❖ *The mandatory waiting period in connection with ABC license transfers is a minimum 30 days, from notice publication to closing, but the ABC Board usually requires at least 60 days to conduct its investigation of the buyer and the transfer application.*

❖ *During this waiting period, it's a good idea for the seller to pay attention to running the business efficiently so everything will be in good order at close of escrow.*

❖ *To the extent possible, parties should avoid talking to customers, employees and others about the planned sale. Of course, you can't be sure your secret will be kept when the fact of the sale has been published in a legal notice newspaper. And certainly, if an ABC transfer is planned, you can't hide that intent, because the state requires that a big poster be attached to the window of the establishment so it can be read from the outside. Still, the less said, the better. At least until the transfer is completed.*

❖ *The waiting period is a good time to plan the transition and prepare a campaign to announce the change to customers.*

❖ *The landlord for the business may be involved in the escrow if he is due to receive a sum equal to the increase in the lease deposit or to a rent hike.*

❖ *Upon closing, the escrow holder will need all the funds scheduled to be distributed to the seller and to any other parties or taxing authorities that have to be paid to clear debts and complete the transaction. Also required will be fees for filings and for any unpaid balance of the escrow fee.*

❖ *Prorations will be calculated and distributed by the escrow company, which also is charged with the responsibility of filing any new liens, security agreements and related documents.*

CHAPTER SEVENTEEN

WHY YOU WANT TO HELP YOUR BUYER SUCCEED

At the beginning of the book, sellers were given this recommendation: Prepare yourself intellectually and emotionally for the process of selling your business. And if you've tried to follow that advice, and some of the other ideas presented here – if you have been patient, persistent and realistic, as was suggested, if you have been empathetic enough to understand your business from a buyer's point of view and yet unyielding in your demand that prospective buyers be well qualified and cooperative – this behavior might have brought you to the satisfactory conclusion of a sale at your price and terms. You were successful because of your disciplined application of some of the principles offered in this book, and because you worked hard at getting your business sold. And maybe you had a little luck working for you.

And even though your mission is largely complete, I think it's important that you continue to remain involved with your former company, at least at a minimal level, to make certain the buyer has what you can provide in the way of counsel, suggestions, and maybe an encouraging word, so he or she will be successful with the business.

Is staying in contact with the buyer and keeping half an eye on the business just too much to ask? Is it more than you'd bargained for? After all, you're very likely to be fatigued by all the hard work and aggravation you endured in the long process of selling your small California business. And now, after a few weeks of what may feel like a forced marriage with the buyer, you might be feeling sick and tired of the whole thing.

Besides, you may have started to notice that the buyer doesn't always pay attention when you're offering up the valuable bits of wisdom gained during your extensive history with the company. He or she may not be heeding all of your advice, sometimes preferring to pursue their own foolish ideas. Well, it's the buyer's business now; the buyer's resource to build, to learn with, to succeed with on his or her terms.

From my experience as a seller, a buyer and a broker, I've come to understand how you might be tempted to put the entire episode behind you and leave the buyer to work things out without your assistance, once your deal is complete and the training period has passed. I've even witnessed situations in which a buyer and seller came to dislike and to distrust one another.

And yet, to the extent possible, I urge new sellers to maintain the patient attitude, and the understanding perspective that has served you–even when you had to grit your teeth and smile – throughout the process of selling your business.

Stay in touch

Don't abandon the buyer, even if you feel uncomfortable about calling periodically or dropping by the place of business. It demonstrates good faith and helps you to remain aware of what's happening with the business.

I'm familiar with a seller, named George, who put his California-based custom fixtures manufacturing company on the market when business was at its best. That was in the late 1990s. But his buyer relations skills weren't as sharp as his business timing because when the recession of 2000 impacted the company, this former owner was reluctant to have any contact with the buyer. George feared that he'd have to hear a lot of complaints and he was worried that he might be asked for more lenient terms on the promissory note he'd taken to finance part of the transaction. In fact, when the buyer telephoned, George neglected to take or to return the calls.

The buyer finally reached George and asked his advice about cutting expenses to deal with the business slowdown. George answered that since the training agreement had expired, they shouldn't talk anymore. And then he made another mistake: George told the buyer: "Call my lawyer if you have any other questions or complaints."

Once one lawyer was involved, it took little time to get the buyer's lawyer on the case and soon there was legal action, charging that George had misrepresented the business, had failed to disclose that a sales decline was coming and had neglected to act in good faith when the buyer turned to him for help.

The case finally was settled, but not until each party had paid out thousands in legal fees and, incidentally, also had learned to hate one another.

We'll never know for sure, but my guess is that had George tried to provide some advice and sympathy, he might have saved himself a lot of money and aggravation.

I think there's an important lesson in this story that even extends to deals that were put together without seller financing.

We never know for sure how a deal might turn out. A transaction that seems promising in every respect because the business is healthy and growing and the buyer and seller have a terrific rapport, can suddenly change, due to unanticipated problems – forces beyond the control of the parties involved.

So, as a general rule, I advocate attempting to stay in communication with those you've encountered along the business path. At least, don't alienate others unnecessarily. A small breakdown in conversation can grow to be a draining and demanding problem. And I've seen major difficulties quickly resolved when people can talk to each other about their issues.

There's no guarantee your buyer will be successful with your business. And if he or she runs into problems, it benefits the buyer, and you benefit as well, if you can make yourself available to help the buyer solve them. Even if you're not able to save the buyer from serious problems, the fact that you tried to be of assistance, in good faith, will go a long way toward keeping you out of trouble.

Conclusion

The seller of a business – after months of work and plenty of frustration – may want nothing else at all to do with the buyer or the business, once it's sold and the training is complete. It's normal to feel that way, but your best bet is to continue to be available to the buyer and keep tabs on the fortunes of the business.

CHAPTER EIGHTEEN

WHAT CAN GO WRONG AND WHAT YOU MIGHT BE ABLE TO DO ABOUT IT

Some years ago, the owner of a business I'll call "Albert's Liquors" – to maintain the anonymity of the parties – decided to offer his profitable, Northern California liquor store for sale so that he could retire and move to the mountains with his wife. A very organized person, Albert carefully prepared his business to be marketed. He arranged for a brand new, long term lease, assembled financial information covering several years and showing constant growth in gross revenues and net profits, and he obtained an appraisal of his equipment – the coolers, cash registers, counters and other fixtures. He discussed the plan with his banker and found out exactly how much the bank would lend toward the purchase price and what qualifications and financial strength would be required of a borrower/buyer. Albert then cleaned the place, top to bottom, got rid of old and outdated inventory, had the walls painted and the carpets replaced. He also put in modern lighting where the old fluorescent fixtures had been.

Albert ordered, and paid for business valuations from two separate appraisal companies and took the average $320,000 plus inventory as his offering price. He held a meeting with all employees so everyone would be aware of what was happening and there would be no secrets to keep.

He even visited the local ABC office and got a packet of information he could show to interested buyers who wanted more details about obtaining his license, should they want to buy his store.

Albert engaged a well-known business broker in the area who was familiar with ABC transfers and he then sat back and waited for the showings to begin, followed by the offers. He was pleased that he'd thought of everything.

Yes, Albert was prepared for a prompt sale at his reasonable price and terms.

The listing was introduced on a Tuesday afternoon. Just hours later, early on Wednesday morning, a young man was murdered in the store's parking lot, victim of a drive-by shooting. It was the first violent crime in this quiet working-class neighborhood in several years. The next day, a police inspector told a reporter for the local newspaper that it appeared a gang war was moving into the area and that officials were preparing for other crimes of this type.

Albert's story is the most dramatic example I know of to illustrate the way unexpected events can impact the efforts to sell a small California business. And he did come up with a strategy that helped get a sale. I'll let you know what happened at the end of this chapter.

Fortunately, most sellers don't have problems of this magnitude. In fact, when feeling badly about your problems, it may help to remember Albert, and to take some comfort in knowing things could be worse. And it serves as a reminder to plan as thoroughly as possible to eliminate any potential problems you can anticipate, then get ready to be flexible if you're impacted by an unexpected occurrence for which you could not have prepared.

The kind of surprise Albert experienced when his store went on the market is actually pretty rare. And there probably is no way you have time and resources to prepare for every one-chance-in-a-million event that you can conjure up as a possibility.

Problems that come packaged as surprises to sellers trying to find buyers for their businesses are more commonly found in these parts of the process: unqualified buyers who swim through the net, complications during the due diligence phase, unexpected claims in escrow, and a change of circumstances impacting the business after the buyer takes over.

Here's what these problems can look like and how you might deal with them.

An Unqualified Buyer

Despite careful precautions sellers can discover they are dealing with a "buyer" who is excited about the business, easy to get along with – perhaps even charming – but somehow can't seem to get it together on the money part of the equation. The buyer may tell you that he is eager to purchase your business and thinks your price and terms are quite reasonable. He can explain the delay in coming up with your down payment as an error at his bank, or the computer malfunction at the brokerage house where his stock was to be sold. He might even complain about the check getting lost in the mail.

Some buyer pretenders can readily be found out. I'm aware of a prospect who produced a banker recommendation on a phony-looking letter head for a non-existent financial institution. Another submitted a financial statement so poorly prepared that the addition was incorrect. But others are very good at deception and it may take awhile before the "beast is unmasked."

Your first line of defense against dishonest buyers is the intuition you've developed in your business career. Most likely you have a sense that something is amiss when someone is attempting to defraud you. Nearly all successful business people develop this ability. The problem with eager sellers, of course, is that they sometimes ignore that "internal" voice which keeps trying to get their attention to let them know they are being conned. We're so pleased to find a buyer who wants exactly what we're selling, and who is so nice about it, that we forget to conduct the gut check to determine if it feels like the person is for real.

Just as buyers are conditioned to approach each new business offering with some natural skepticism and caution, you should regard every buyer you first meet as a bit suspicious until he or she proves to be reliable. Make sure to dole out information slowly and carefully in return for the buyer's disclosures. This is the dance that was discussed in an earlier chapter.

And it's very important that you maintain your file of prospective buyers so that if your favorite candidate seems to be long on conversation but short on cash, you'll be in a position to get other buyers interested in your offering. Soliciting back up offers should be part of the strategy in the campaign to sell your small California business. And make certain that all buyers are aware of this. If they want the business, they'll have to be prepared to deal quickly and honestly.

Due Diligence Delays and Disturbances

There's an inverse relationship between the amount of preparation that goes into getting your business ready for sale, and the likelihood that new and damaging information about it will come up while the buyer is conducting a due diligence examination of your company.

That means if you've completed the job of assembling your financial and other documents, and if you've talked to your landlord, franchisor, banker and accountant about all of the issues that could come up, then double checked to make sure your company is in compliance with the latest regulations, you have reduced the likelihood that there are any problems lurking in the background, waiting to be discovered by a buyer who is analyzing your business before removing the final contingencies.

Most likely, if there is a concern expressed by the buyer, it will be over something for which you are prepared – that is, if you've practiced clear and consistent communications with the buyer – and if you've reminded him or her to maintain realistic expectations.

"Yes, it's true that this could be a problem," you can tell the buyer who's worried about a competitor moving into the area, or a key employee who might quit, or an increase in costs from one of your important vendors. "And now," you go on to explain, "let's talk about how to overcome this temporary challenge."

There is no reason for you or your buyer to panic every time a new difficulty makes an appearance in the constant parade of challenges that face nearly all business owners. If you don't over react to the issue, the buyer will probably be reassured that there are solutions to this and to many other problems that you face every day, and that he or she can expect to face on a regular basis, once taking over as new owner of the business.

And if you and your buyer become aware of some startling new development that might threaten the well-being of your company even if it were not sold, there may be a way to restructure your deal to accommodate this major problem. I've talked about some of these solutions in a previous chapter.

The worst thing you can do, as a seller during the due diligence period, is to let a new factor – large or small – cause serious delays in your progress toward close of escrow. Keep the deal moving however you can, because once a transaction becomes "stalled," it takes enormous energy to get it started up again – if it can be revitalized at all.

Escrow Surprises

Among the most annoying discoveries in the process of selling your business is that there's a claim in escrow from someone you've never heard of, or who was paid off a long time ago. And then there's the legitimate claim from a lien holder who you simply forgot about.

I classify these as annoyances because they're rarely deal killers. Speed bumps in the road to a completed escrow simply confuse the buyer – perhaps causing him or her to entertain second thoughts about the choice to purchase your business.

Rightful claims that somehow did not get handled before you took your business to market should be taken care of now. Small items can usually be dispatched quickly. One seller was sure she'd paid off a vendor who put a claim for about $100 into the escrow. Rather than waste the time and energy trying to dispute the claim, however, she simply agreed to have it paid again out of the proceeds. Then the buyer put another $50 into the deal, wanting to split the expense as a gesture of goodwill toward the seller.

And if the claim involves a lot of money, you can always agree to have the transaction close on time, with the disputed sums held back in escrow until the issue is resolved. Any false claim from a broker or from anyone else who wants to profit from your deal but can't prove a right to do so, will be quickly dismissed. You might even have the opportunity to take the claimant to court – if you want – and request that you be awarded damages.

Again, the priority is to keep your deal moving forward toward the close, and to communicate with the buyer and the escrow holder about how to best handle any claims or other actions that threaten to delay the completion of your deal.

Major Changes After Sale

And suppose your buyer takes over and has problems keeping the business functioning at a profitable level. This might be the result of a buyer who is unable to manage the business, keep customers happy, work with suppliers and provide competent supervision and leadership for employees. Or it could be the consequence of a dramatic change in the market or the composition of the industry.

What's your role? Well, there is only so much you can do about this. You might be able to provide some assistance, as recommended in the previous chapter. But the business now belongs to the buyer. The problem belongs primarily to the buyer.

The failing business is your problem only to the extent that it represents security for the obligation owed to you by the buyer, and if the business is the only collateral. And your liability exposure in a legal sense is limited if you were careful, during the marketing and sale of your business, to tell the truth, to provide as much information as possible, and to keep track of what happened with notes and copies of documents in your file.

There is no guarantee that the buyer will be successful. And no guarantee that if he or she begins to fail, you won't be asked to contribute to a "bail-out," either by invitation to participate in retroactive negotiations or with a law suit that claims you created, withheld or misrepresented the facts about the business.

If you remain aware of the fact that once in awhile the sale of a small California businesses leads to unfortunate consequences, such as a failing company, you will be reminded to use caution and intelligence at every step of the process. And apply some of the ideas presented in these pages.

Make sure you start with a qualified buyer, supply all relevant information, negotiate for the best arrangement that gets you a deal, share with the buyer your view of realistic expectations for the business, offer to help when appropriate, and keep notes and documents that provide a record of your words and actions. These strategies will help keep your loss to a minimum in the event your buyer doesn't achieve the success you had with the business.

Albert's Solution

This chapter opened with the story of Albert who did most everything a seller can to prepare his small California business for the market and still suffered the effects of a devastating occurrence, outside of his control and severely impacting his ability to sell. To solve the problem, Albert took the liquor store off the market, hired a security company to patrol the property and then, about nine months later, again offered the store for sale – this time at a lower price. The value of the business was hurt by the poor publicity, a decline in business and the added drain on profits represented by the cost of the security guards. Albert was able to get an accepted offer and a closed deal at about half the price requested originally.

Conclusion

When owners prepare their small California businesses for sale, put them on the market, negotiate their deals, close their escrows and deal with the aftermath of a sale, if any, they are advised to prepare carefully and thoroughly so their plans won't be ruined by unanticipated occurrences. But conducting business – just like living – is full of surprises. It's your job as a seller to try and apply what precautions you can to prevent problems, and to use your intelligence and creativity when you are called on to deal with the unexpected.

KEY POINTS FROM THIS CHAPTER

❖ *The story of Albert's Liquors illustrates that even with the best laid plans there is no guarantee that things will work as anticipated. Unexpected occurrences remind us that we don't have control over all the factors.*

❖ *Sellers sometimes are charmed by an unqualified buyer who is long on conversation; short on cash. One way for a seller to be alerted to the possibility that a buyer has ulterior motives is to pay attention to your instincts about the person. You often can trust the innate ability to "read" people, developed over years of conducting business. Don't let your eagerness to sell, overcome your good judgment.*

❖ *It's important to maintain your file of prospective buyers – even when there's an accepted offer – so that you can seek back up offers.*

❖ *A business well prepared for sale should yield no deal-killing surprises when examined by a buyer during a due diligence evaluation. To minimize the impact of any problems discovered by a buyer, its best to prepare the buyer to have realistic expectations and to reassure a buyer that minor problems don't cause major business disruptions.*

❖ *Unanticipated claims that appear in escrow are usually more an annoyance than a deal wrecker. Communicating with the escrow company as to how to deal with the claims is often a useful solution. Escrow can set aside money for the large claims to be dealt with later, and the deal can close as scheduled.*

❖ *It is very important to keep a deal moving forward at any and all stages. Delays and stalls can kill a transaction. Sellers are advised to do whatever needed to maintain the momentum from accepted offer to closed escrow.*

❖ *There is not a lot a seller can do for a buyer who's running the business poorly or encountering major difficulties unexpected before the deal closed. If the buyer is open to suggestion, perhaps the seller can offer advice.*

❖ *Sellers are advised to be aware of the worst that can happen in a deal and let that be a reminder to follow the advice offered in these pages, so as to minimize your exposure to financial loss and to charges that you misled the buyer.*

❖ *It's a good idea, and often repeated in this book, to maintain a file with notes and documents that can demonstrate what you said and did during the whole process of marketing and selling your business and closing the deal.*

AFTERWORD

Rather than conclude on a negative note – with the last chapter devoted to the things that can go wrong – I want to end these pages with a suggestion about how the seller of a small California business can gain value from this book.

In my seminars and consulting assignments, I've learned that some of the ideas and suggestions I offer are considered by some sellers to be very elementary; almost too obvious to deserve mention. Other sellers find these same concepts to be very useful and precisely applicable to their situations, as if I'd hit on exactly an issue with which they were having difficulties.

My audience for this work is very broad, consisting of people from most every kind of background represented in our state's diverse population – the diverse population, incidentally, that makes California such a great place in which to live and to conduct business.

Whether you have found the information contained in these pages to be a reminder about principles you already know, or you have discovered a few new ideas, or this book is your first formal introduction to the subject of selling your business, I mean for you to gain not only practical advice, but also an overall understanding of how to be successful in selling your small California business.

As we've noted, most small California businesses that go on the market never are sold. You can beat these odds by the proper use of these tools and strategies, and by applying the qualities in your thinking and in your actions which make up the subtext of this book, and which I believe are just as necessary as the specific ideas. I've noticed that successful sellers are not only consistent in applying these how-to tips, they also are open to ideas, responsive to the marketplace, creative in the search for solutions to problems, honest and communicative with their advisors and colleagues, and they're realistic about the expectations they have for themselves and for this process.

My hope for you is that your investment in buying and reading this book will pay off in your achievement of a successful sale of your business.

INDEX

Featuring the Successful bizben Method!